March 2012

SECURITIES INVESTOR PROTECTION CORPORATION

Interim Report on the Madoff Liquidation Proceeding

GAO
Accountability ★ Integrity ★ Reliability

GAO-12-414

GAO
Accountability * Integrity * Reliability

Highlights

Highlights of GAO-12-414, a report to congressional requesters

SECURITIES INVESTOR PROTECTION CORPORATION

Interim Report on the Madoff Liquidation Proceeding

Why GAO Did This Study

With the collapse of Bernard L. Madoff Investment Securities, LLC—a broker-dealer and investment advisory firm with thousands of clients—Bernard Madoff admitted to reporting $57.2 billion in fictitious customer holdings. The Securities Investor Protection Corporation (SIPC), which oversees a fund providing up to $500,000 of protection to qualifying individual customers of failed securities firms, selected a trustee to liquidate the Madoff firm and recover assets for its investors. The method the Trustee is using to determine how much a customer filing a claim could be eligible to recover—an amount known as "net equity"—has been the subject of dispute and litigation. This report discusses (1) how the Trustee and trustee's counsel were selected, (2) why the method for valuing customer claims was chosen, (3) costs of the liquidation, and (4) disclosures the Trustee has made about its progress. GAO examined the Securities Investor Protection Act; court filings and decisions; and SIPC, Securities and Exchange Commission (SEC), and Trustee reports and records. GAO analyzed cost filings and interviewed SIPC, SEC, and SEC Inspector General officials, and the Trustee and his counsel.

What GAO Recommends

SEC should advise SIPC to (1) document its procedures for identifying candidates for trustee or trustee's counsel, and in so doing, to assess whether additional outreach efforts should be incorporated, and (2) document a process and criteria for appointment of a trustee and trustee's counsel. SEC and SIPC concurred with our recommendations.

View GAO-12-414. For more information, contact A. Nicole Clowers at (202) 512-8678 or clowersa@gao.gov.

What GAO Found

The Securities Investor Protection Corporation (SIPC) generally followed its past practices in selecting the trustee for the Madoff liquidation. SIPC maintains a file of trustee candidates from across the country, but given the anticipated complexities of the case, officials said the field of potential qualified trustees was limited. SIPC has sole discretion to appoint trustees and, wanting to act quickly, SIPC senior management considered four trustee candidates. After three of the four candidates were eliminated for reasons including having a conflict of interest or ongoing work on a large financial firm failure, SIPC selected Irving H. Picard, who has considerable securities and trustee experience. However, SIPC has not documented a formal outreach procedure for identifying candidates for trustee and trustee's counsel, or documented its procedures and criteria for selecting persons for particular cases, as internal control standards recommend. Having such documented procedures could allow SIPC to better assess whether it has identified an optimal pool of candidates, and to enhance the transparency of its selection decisions.

A key goal of broker-dealer liquidations is to provide customers with the securities or cash they had in their accounts. However, because the Trustee determined that amounts shown on Madoff customers' statements reflected years of fictitious investments and profits, he chose to determine customers' net equity using the "net investment method" (NIM), which values customer claims based on amounts invested, less amounts withdrawn. SIPC senior management and officials of the Securities and Exchange Commission (SEC)—which oversees SIPC—initially agreed on the appropriateness of NIM. Over the course of 2009, however, SEC officials continued to consider alternative approaches for reimbursing customers. Although some customers have challenged the Trustee's use of NIM, two courts have held that the Trustee's approach is consistent with the law and with past cases, with both courts indicating that using the values shown on customers' final statements would effectively sanction the Madoff fraud and produce "absurd" results. In November 2009, SEC commissioners voted to support the use of NIM, but with an adjustment for inflation, in an approach known as the "constant dollar" method. However, after an SEC official's conflict of interest was made public in February 2011, the SEC Chairman directed SEC staff to review whether the commission should revote on the constant dollar approach. The matter is currently pending.

As of October 2011, costs of the Madoff liquidation reached more than $450 million, and the Trustee estimates the total costs will exceed $1 billion by 2014. Legal costs, which include costs for the Trustee and the trustee's counsel, are the largest category. While the estimated total cost for the Madoff liquidation is double the total for all completed SIPC cases to date, the Trustee, SIPC, and SEC note that the costs reflect the unprecedented size, duration, and complexity of the Madoff fraud. SIPC senior management also said the liquidation costs are justified, as litigation the trustee has pursued has produced $8.7 billion in recoveries for customers to date. Through various reports, court filings, and a website, the Trustee has disclosed information about the status of the liquidation. SIPC senior management, SEC officials, and the U.S. Bankruptcy Court have concluded that the Trustee's disclosures sufficiently address the requirements for disclosure under the Bankruptcy Code and the Securities Investor Protection Act.

_____ United States Government Accountability Office

Contents

Figures

Abbreviations

ABA	American Bar Association
Baker Hostetler	Baker & Hostetler LLP
FSM	final statement method
NIM	net investment method
SEC	Securities and Exchange Commission
SEC IG	Securities and Exchange Commission Office of Inspector General
SIPA	Securities Investor Protection Act of 1970
SIPC	Securities Investor Protection Corporation
Treasury	Department of the Treasury

United States Government Accountability Office
Washington, DC 20548

March 7, 2012

The Honorable Scott Garrett
Subcommittee on Capital Markets
 and Government Sponsored Enterprises
Committee on Financial Services
House of Representatives

The Honorable Peter King
House of Representatives

The Honorable Carolyn McCarthy
House of Representatives

The Honorable Ileana Ros-Lehtinen
House of Representatives

With the collapse of Bernard L. Madoff Investment Securities, LLC—a broker-dealer and investment advisory firm with thousands of clients—in December 2008, Bernard Madoff admitted to crafting fictitious trades and account statements that showed customer investments totaling $57.2 billion. After the fraud was disclosed, investigators found no securities were ever purchased for customers. Within days of Madoff's arrest, the Securities Investor Protection Corporation (SIPC), a nonprofit, nongovernmental membership corporation responsible for providing financial protection to customers of failed securities firms, put the Madoff firm into liquidation. As part of this process, SIPC designated a trustee, attorney Irving H. Picard (referred to as the Trustee throughout this report), to oversee the liquidation of the firm and recover assets for the benefit of investors.

The Securities Investor Protection Act of 1970 (SIPA) established procedures for liquidating failed broker-dealers. In a liquidation under SIPA, the trustee establishes a fund of customer property consisting of the cash and securities held by the broker-dealer on behalf of customers, plus any assets recovered by the trustee, for distribution among customers. Amounts in this customer property fund generally are distributed to the firm's customers according to the value of their account holdings, known as "net equity." Determination of net equity is a crucial step in settling customer claims for reimbursement from the SIPC fund and distributing any assets recovered from a firm's liquidation. According to SIPC, in a typical case, net equity is based on amounts reflected on statements from the broker-dealer firm to the customer, in what is known as the "final statement method" (FSM). In the Madoff case, however, the Trustee said he determined that securities positions shown on customer statements were fictitious. Thus, he decided to value each customer's net equity according to the amount of cash deposited less any amounts withdrawn—a method known as the "net investment method" (NIM). As a result, not all customers are eligible to receive funds from the liquidation. Further, the Trustee has also been pursuing lawsuits, known as "avoidance" or "clawback" actions, to recover funds from customers who withdrew more from their accounts than they had invested.[1] SIPC senior management and officials of the Securities and Exchange Commission (SEC), which has oversight responsibilities for SIPC, told us they supported the Trustee's decision to use NIM.

Because of the importance of the decision to use NIM in determining customer claims, you asked us to examine a series of questions about the actions of SIPC, the Trustee, and SEC as they relate to this decision. This report discusses (1) how the Trustee and trustee's legal counsel were selected for the Madoff liquidation, (2) the process and reasoning for the selection of NIM in determining customer claims, (3) the costs of the Madoff liquidation, and (4) the information that the Trustee has disclosed about his investigation and activities. You also asked us to examine additional issues related to the Madoff liquidation, which we will address in a future report, as agreed with your offices.[2]

For this report, we reviewed SIPA's requirements, analyzed SIPC procedures for trustee selection, and compared the process for selecting the trustee for the Madoff liquidation with past cases. We also examined how and why the Trustee selected NIM as the method for determining customer net equity, including comparing the selection of NIM in this case to the methods used in other SIPC Ponzi scheme cases.[3] We analyzed and summarized court decisions related to the Madoff liquidation and selection of NIM. We also analyzed costs of the Madoff liquidation, as

---

[1]Avoidance, or clawback, actions enable a bankruptcy trustee to recover for the bankrupt estate certain payments made by the debtor prior to the bankruptcy filing.

[2]We expect our future work will include, among other things, issues relating to customer claims and the Trustee's asset recovery actions.

[3]A Ponzi scheme is an investment fraud that involves the payment of purported returns to existing investors from funds contributed by new investors.

reported by the Trustee, and examined SIPC and Trustee procedures for reviewing and controlling liquidation costs. We assessed the cost data to the extent necessary and deemed it sufficiently reliable for our purposes of identifying total costs, cost components, and trends. We examined SIPA requirements for information disclosures that trustees must make, and reviewed disclosures the Trustee has made to date. Finally, we interviewed officials from SIPC, SEC, and the SEC Office of Inspector General, plus the Trustee and his counsel. See appendix I for additional information on our scope and methodology.

We conducted this performance audit from October 2011 to March 2012 in accordance with generally accepted government auditing standards. Those standards require that we plan and perform the audit to obtain sufficient, appropriate evidence to provide a reasonable basis for our findings and conclusions based on our audit objectives. We believe that the evidence obtained provides a reasonable basis for our findings and conclusions based on our audit objectives.

Background

SIPC's mission is to promote confidence in securities markets by seeking to return customers' cash and securities when a broker-dealer fails. SIPC provides advances for these customers up to the SIPA protection limits—$500,000 per customer, except that claims for cash are limited to $250,000 per customer.[4] SIPC is governed by a seven-member board of directors. Its membership is, generally, brokers or dealers registered under section 15(b) of the Securities and Exchange Act of 1934. Membership is mandatory for all registered broker-dealers that do not meet one of the limited statutory exemptions.[5] As of December 31, 2010, SIPC had 4,773 members.

While SIPC is not a federal agency, it is subject to federal oversight. Under SIPA, SEC exercises what the U.S. Supreme Court has

---

[4]The cash limitation amount is subject to potential adjustment for inflation every 5 years. According to SIPC, the $500,000 limit for securities, rather than the limit for cash, applied in the Madoff liquidation. At the start of the Madoff case, the cash protection limit was $100,000 per customer.

[5]15 U.S.C. § 78ccc(a)(2)(A). This provision exempts certain categories of brokers and dealers, including those whose principal business is conducted outside of the United States.

recognized as "plenary," or general, supervisory authority over SIPC.[6] Specifically, SIPC bylaws and rules are subject to SEC review. SEC also may require SIPC to adopt, amend, or repeal any bylaw or rule. In addition, SEC can participate as a party in any judicial proceeding under SIPA and can file an application in the U.S. District Court for the District of Columbia for an order compelling SIPC to carry out its statutory obligations. Further, SIPA authorizes SEC to conduct inspections and examinations of SIPC, and requires SIPC to furnish SEC with reports and records that it believes are necessary or appropriate in the public interest or to fulfill the purposes of SIPA. All seven members of SIPC's board of directors are appointed by federal officials: one is appointed by the Secretary of the Treasury and one by the Federal Reserve Board, from among the officers and employees of those agencies, and five are appointed by the President, subject to Senate confirmation.[7]

SIPC Fund

SIPA established a fund (SIPC fund) to pay for SIPC's operations and activities. SIPC uses the fund to make advances to satisfy customer claims for missing cash and securities, including notes, stocks, bonds, and certificates of deposit. The SIPC fund also covers the administrative expenses of a liquidation proceeding when the general estate of the failed firm is insufficient; these include costs incurred by a trustee, trustee's counsel, and other advisors.[8]

SIPC finances the fund through annual assessments, set by SIPC, on all member firms, plus interest generated from its investments in Department of the Treasury (Treasury) notes. If the SIPC fund becomes, or appears to be, insufficient to carry out the purposes of SIPA, SIPC can borrow up to $2.5 billion from the Treasury through SEC, whereby SEC would borrow the funds from the Treasury and relend them to SIPC. Figure 1 shows the SIPC fund's balance over the past decade, with the balance falling after the 2008 financial crisis and beginning to recover in 2010.

---

[6]*Securities Investor Protection Corporation v. Barbour*, 421 U.S. 412, 417 (1975).

[7]15 U.S.C. § 78ccc(c)(2). Three of the presidential appointees come from the securities industry. The other two are members of the general public not associated with the securities industry for at least 2 years preceding their appointment. The President designates the chair and vice chair from among the general public members.

[8]In this report, we generally use "costs" to include fees, such as hourly billings for attorneys, as well as other expenses incurred.

Figure 1: SIPC Fund Balance, from 2000 through 2010

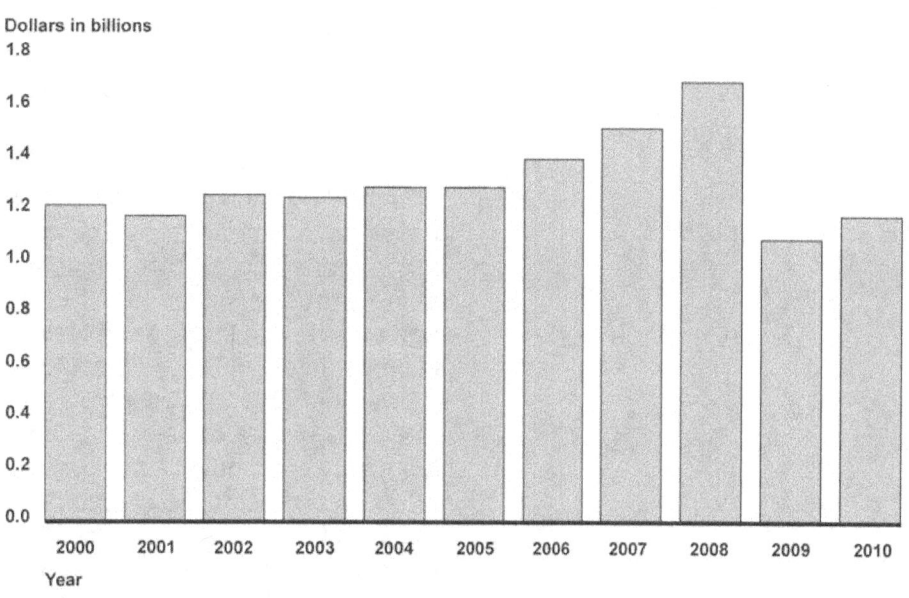

Source: SIPC.

According to SIPC senior management, recent demands on the fund, including from the Madoff case, coupled with a change in SIPC bylaws increasing the target size of the fund from $1 billion to $2.5 billion, led SIPC to impose new industry assessments that total about $400 million annually. The assessments, equal to one-quarter of 1 percent of net operating revenue, will continue until the $2.5 billion target is reached, according to SIPC senior management. The new assessments replaced a flat $150 annual assessment per member firm.[9] Under the new levies, the average assessment for 2010 was $91,755 per firm, with a median of $2,095, according to SIPC. See appendix II for a history of assessments and assessment rates for the SIPC fund.

[9]In March 2009, SIPC announced that it was increasing the assessment, effective April 1, 2009, after determining, pursuant to SIPA and SIPC bylaws, that the fund balance was "reasonably likely" to remain less than $1 billion for at least 6 months.

Liquidations under SIPA

SIPA authorizes SIPC to begin a liquidation action by applying for a protective order from an appropriate federal district court if it determines that one of its member broker-dealers has failed or is in danger of failing to meet its obligations to customers and one or more additional statutory conditions are met.[10] The broker-dealer has an opportunity to contest the protective order application. If the court issues the order, the court appoints a "disinterested" trustee selected by SIPC, or, in certain cases, SIPC itself, to liquidate the firm.[11] Under SIPA, SIPC has sole discretion to select a trustee and trustee's counsel for the liquidation of a member broker-dealer firm. SEC has no statutory role in the selection of the trustee or trustee's counsel. SIPC attempts to match the size of the engagement with the capabilities of service providers. If SIPC were not to act immediately, SEC could opt to seek court appointment of an SEC receiver, pending SIPC action, according to SIPC senior management. After SIPC makes its selection and the trustee is appointed, the bankruptcy court holds a disinterestedness hearing, at which interested parties can object to the selected individual and firm named as counsel. The district court also orders removal of the liquidation proceeding to the federal bankruptcy court for that district. To the extent that it is consistent with SIPA, the proceeding is conducted pursuant to provisions of the Bankruptcy Code.

While SIPC designates the trustee, that person, once judicially appointed, becomes an officer of the court. As such, the trustee exercises independent judgment and does not serve as an agent of SIPC. Indeed, SIPC-designated trustees and SIPC have occasionally taken opposing legal

---

[10]For SIPC to initiate a proceeding, at least one of the following other factors must exist: (1) the firm must be insolvent under the Bankruptcy Code or unable to meet its obligations as they become due; (2) the firm is subject to a court or agency proceeding in which a receiver, liquidator, or trustee has been appointed; (3) the firm is not compliant with applicable requirements under the Securities Exchange Act of 1934 or financial responsibility rules of SEC or financial self-regulatory organizations; or (4) the firm is unable to show compliance with such rules. In the smallest proceedings (in which, among other factors, the claims of all customers are less than $250,000), SIPC may directly pay customer claims without filing an application for a protective decree with a court and without the appointment of a trustee.

[11]Disinterested means, among other things, that the trustee has no outstanding financial obligation with the failed firm or has not been employed or acted as attorney for the firm within the last 2 years.

positions in liquidation proceedings.[12] Under SIPA, the trustee must investigate facts and circumstances relating to the liquidation; report to the court facts indicating fraud, misconduct, mismanagement, or irregularities; and submit a final report to SIPC and others designated by the court. Also, the trustee is to periodically report to the court and SIPC on his or her progress in distributing cash and securities to customers. The bankruptcy court is to grant the trustee and trustee's counsel "reasonable compensation" for services rendered and reimbursement for proper costs and expenses incurred in connection with the liquidation proceeding.[13]

Promptly after being appointed, the trustee must publish a notice of the proceeding in one or more major newspapers, in a form and manner determined by the court. The trustee also must see that a copy of the notice is mailed to existing and recent customers listed on the broker-dealer's books and records, and provide notice to creditors in the manner the Bankruptcy Code prescribes. Customers must file written statements of claims. The notice typically informs customers how to file claims and explains deadlines. Two deadlines apply. One is set by the bankruptcy court supervising the proceeding, and the other by SIPA. The bankruptcy court deadline for filing customer claims applies to customer claims for net equity and may not exceed 60 days after the date that notice of the proceeding is published. Failure to meet the deadline can affect whether a customer claim is satisfied with securities or cash in lieu of securities. The SIPA deadline occurs 6 months after the publication date. SIPA mandates that the trustee cannot allow any customer or general creditor claim received after the 6-month deadline, except claims filed by the United States, any state or local government, or certain infants and incompetent persons (although a request for an extension must be filed before the 6-month period has lapsed).

Once filed, claims undergo various review, according to the Trustee. First, the Trustee's claims agent reviews claims for completeness; if information

---

[12]See, for example, *Securities Investor Protection Corp. v. Morgan, Kennedy & Co., Inc.*, 533 F.2d 1314 (2d Cir. 1976); *SEC v. Wick*, 360 F. Supp. 312 (N.D. Ill. 1973); *In re Bell and Beckwith*, 93 B.R. 569 (Bankr. N.D. Ohio 1988).

[13]15 U.S.C. § 78eee(b)(5)(A). In addition to the use of designated counsel, SIPA trustees generally are authorized, with SIPC approval, to hire and fix the compensation of personnel necessary to carry out liquidations, including officers and employees of the debtor and its examining authority, as well as accountants, and to use the services of SIPC employees. 15 U.S.C. § 78fff-1(a)(1), (2).

is found to be missing, the claims agent sends a request for additional information. Next, the Trustee's forensic accountants review each claim form, information gathered from the Madoff firm's records regarding the account at issue, and information submitted directly by the claimant. The Trustee uses the results of this review in assessing his determination of the claim. Finally, claims move to SIPC, where a claims review specialist provides a recommendation to the Trustee on how each claim should be determined. Once that recommendation has been made, the Trustee and trustee's counsel review it, as well as legal or other issues raised previously. When the Trustee has decided on resolution of a claim, he issues a determination letter to the claimant. The letter also informs claimants of their right to object to the determination and how to do so. The bankruptcy court judge overseeing the liquidation rules on a customer's objections after holding a hearing on the matter. Decisions of the bankruptcy court may be appealed to the appropriate federal district court, and then upward through the federal appellate process. As of January 27, 2012, the Trustee had received 16,519 customer claims in the Madoff proceeding, and reached determinations on all but two of them.

Figure 2 shows a timeline of key events in the Madoff liquidation.

Figure 2: Key Events in the Madoff Liquidation, December 2008 to January 2012

12/11: Madoff arrested, criminally charged with multibillion-dollar fraud.

12/15: U.S. District Court appoints Irving Picard as trustee to liquidate Madoff firm, and law firm Baker & Hostetler as trustee's counsel.

3/12: Madoff pleads guilty to 11 counts, including criminal fraud and money laundering.

7/29: Trustee files lawsuit against Ruth Madoff, wife of Bernard Madoff, seeking $45 million.

10/2: Trustee files lawsuit against four Madoff family members, seeking $200 million.

10/28: SIPC advances reach $500 million, exceeding total of all prior cases.

11/26: Trustee files 40 lawsuits against relatives of Madoff and wife, plus former employees and relatives, seeking $69 million.

6/28: Bankruptcy court rules against investors in "feeder funds"—companies that raised money and placed funds with Madoff firm—on claim that such investors should be treated as individual Madoff customers.

1/17: Trustee report on progress to date: recoveries/ settlements at $8.7 billion; customer distributions at $325.5 million; and SIPC advances at $797.8 million.

2009

2010

2011

2012

1/2: Claim forms mailed to Madoff customers.

3/2: Securities Investor Protection Corporation (SIPC) announces reinstatement of assessments on operating revenues of member firms, to build SIPC fund.

8/5: SIPC agrees to pay undisputed portion of claims up to coverage limit even if customer has objected to Trustee's determination of a claim.

7/2: Period to submit claims ends.

6/29: Madoff sentenced to maximum of 150 years in prison.

3/1: Addressing key issue, bankruptcy court upholds Trustee's method for determining value of customer claims.

12/17: In largest recovery, Trustee and U.S. Department of Justice announce $7.2 billion settlement with Picower estate, with $5 billion allotted to customer fund.

8/16: U.S. Court of Appeals upholds Trustee's method for determining value of customer claims.

10/5: First distribution to customers—$312 million—begins.

11/22: Trustee reaches $326 million settlement with Internal Revenue Service to recover taxes paid on behalf of account holders, allegedly to make Ponzi scheme appear authentic.

Source: GAO summary of SIPC and court records.

Note: Some amounts may be approximate.

SIPC Says It Followed Its Normal Process in Selecting the Trustee, but Lacks Documented Procedures and Formal Outreach

A SIPC liquidation of a member broker-dealer begins when either SEC or a securities self-regulatory organization, such as the Financial Industry Regulatory Authority, recommends that a firm's failure may require SIPC assistance, usually because of theft or other misuse of customer assets and insolvency. If SIPC's president, general counsel, and vice president for operations agree that a case should be opened, the SIPC president requests authority from the SIPC board chair to begin the action.

Upon receiving this authority, the SIPC president selects a trustee and trustee's counsel after consultation within SIPC. According to SIPC senior management, the SIPC board does not vote on the selections. Instead, the selection relies on the judgment of SIPC senior management in what they describe as a relatively narrow field of specialty. SIPC senior management told us they attempt to match the size of the liquidation proceeding with the capabilities of the individuals and firms that will perform the liquidation. Typically in SIPC cases, the firm selected to act as the trustee's counsel is the same law firm of which the trustee is a member, and the statute explicitly permits this.[14] According to SIPC senior management, having a trustee from the same law firm increases efficiency and cuts costs, as it provides better communication and allows the trustee to make better use of legal resources.

To assist in selection of a trustee or trustee's counsel, SIPC maintains a file of candidates from across the country, which contains information such as professional experience and billing rates, and it subscribes to an information service that provides background information and ratings on lawyers and law firms, and identifies areas of specialization. SIPC informally assembles its roster from multiple sources, including inquiries from firms interested in SIPC business and SIPC's experience with firms it encounters in legal proceedings. Where SIPC is unfamiliar with local practitioners, it will seek recommendations from SEC staff and local judges. Among firms new to its roster, SIPC seeks to build their experience by using them as trustee's counsel in relatively small cases in which SIPC itself acts as trustee, or by having them serve as counsel in matters in which the SIPA trustee or trustee's counsel discover during an investigation a previously unknown conflict of interest, according to SIPC senior management. At the conclusion of a case, SIPC senior management prepares a legal and accounting evaluation of service providers used. Included in this evaluation is a recommendation whether to use the service provider again. If SIPC staff recommends against a provider, SIPC senior management told us, the provider is less likely to be selected in the future. We sought to review such evaluations, but SIPC senior management declined to provide them to us on the grounds they cover privileged attorney work-product information.[15]

---

[14]The statutory provision was adopted in 1978 amendments to SIPA, and SIPC supported the change following inquiries from judges about whether the practice was permissible, according to the SIPC President.

[15]According to SIPC senior management, it is important that SIPC attorneys be free to express candid opinions on quality of services provided.

According to SIPC senior management, the selection of the Madoff trustee followed these past practices. Specifically, according to senior management, the SIPC President received a call from SEC on December 11, 2008, advising him that Madoff had just turned himself in to law enforcement and had admitted to a massive fraud at his firm. Because of the likely size and complexity of this case, SIPC senior management told us that selecting an experienced attorney to act as trustee would be important, which limited the field of potential trustees. Upon learning of the failure of the Madoff firm, SIPC senior management used their experience and judgment to initially identify four potential trustees from their pool of candidates, including Mr. Picard. The three others were a former New York municipal finance official, who was a lawyer and accountant but had not done a SIPC case and was not a member of a law firm; an experienced liquidation attorney who was already busy with another large financial firm failure; and another candidate from a large New York law firm with extensive bankruptcy experience, but that law firm had a disqualifying conflict of interest. Because of the situations of the other candidates, SIPC contacted Mr. Picard on the morning of December 11, 2008, and asked him to serve as trustee for the Madoff liquidation. As described later, the law firm Mr. Picard would soon join, Baker & Hostetler LLP (Baker Hostetler), was named as the trustee's counsel. Similarly, SIPC senior management told us that SIPC followed a similar process in the recent large failure of MF Global, Inc., in which they contacted 5 candidates, drawn from an initial field of about 10, before the selection was made.

Although SIPC senior management said the process in selecting the Madoff trustee followed past selection practices, such practices are not documented. According to SIPC senior management, current SIPC policies do not document the decision process and any criteria applied in making selections because senior managers rely on their judgment and familiarity with individuals with appropriate experience. Further, they noted they must act quickly to get a trustee in place for a failed firm as soon as possible, because broker-dealer firms often fail with little advance warning. Moreover, they said that getting a trustee in place quickly to take over operations of the firm is essential to preserving assets and maximizing returns to customers.

However, federal and private sector standards for internal control recommend that an entity document its system of internal controls, by such means as management directives, policies, operating instructions, and written manuals.[16] In the case of trustee selection, documented policies and criteria would allow SIPC's oversight agency, SEC, to more effectively assess whether SIPC follows consistent practices in selecting trustees, as well as increase the transparency of SIPC's decisionmaking. SEC officials told us that having SIPC better document its selection process would improve SEC's ability to oversee SIPC activities, in such areas as determining the extent to which SIPC considered the fees charged by trustees or how it addressed potential conflict-of-interest situations. SEC officials told us they plan to discuss better documenting the trustee selection process and criteria with SIPC.

SIPC also has not documented its outreach process for identifying potential candidates to serve as trustees. SIPC senior management told us they do not make formal efforts to expand the trustee candidate roster, such as by regularly or systematically identifying or approaching other parties. They said they view such efforts as unnecessary or impractical because the number of attorneys who conduct work relevant to broker-dealer bankruptcies is small enough that SIPC is already is aware of most of them, or the attorneys already are familiar with SIPC. Moreover, according to SIPC senior management, actively soliciting candidates could be burdensome for SIPC, by producing too much information about too many firms that can quickly become outdated. They told us such an undertaking would duplicate information already available through its information service subscription, and that because SIPA liquidations can be infrequent and in more remote areas of the country, it is more efficient to obtain current information on qualified firms through the information service and the firms' websites.

However, undertaking additional efforts to more systematically identify other candidates, and to document this process, could help ensure that the range of choices, which SIPC senior management acknowledges is currently limited to a small group with the requisite skills, reflects the widest capabilities available. Access to a potentially wider pool of candidates could help ensure that SIPC is better equipped to meet its responsibilities. SEC officials told us that SIPC's goal is to use individuals and law firms capable of high-quality work, to avoid potentially damaging legal decisions that could hinder SIPC in future liquidations. Having a

---

[16]See GAO, *Standards for Internal Control in the Federal Government*, GAO/AIMD-00-21.3.1 (Washington, D.C.: November 1999), and Committee of Sponsoring Organizations of the Treadway Commission, *Internal Control - Integrated Framework* (1992).

documented, formal outreach process would allow SEC to better assess whether SIPC's outreach efforts are sufficient for ensuring that SIPC is identifying the optimal pool of candidates. SEC officials told us they likely would discuss with SIPC senior management whether its roster of candidates is sufficiently broad, as a wider pool could preserve quality while offering the opportunity for lowering costs.[17]

The Trustee Has Considerable Experience

The trustee that SIPC selected for the Madoff liquidation has considerable industry and broker-dealer liquidation experience. He served as the first U.S. Trustee for the Southern District of New York, where his duties included appointing and supervising trustees who administer consumer debtors' bankruptcy estates and corporate reorganization cases, and who litigate bankruptcy related matters. He appointed the trustee for reorganization of O.P.M. Leasing Services, Inc., a several-hundred-million-dollar Ponzi scheme case involving nonexistent computer equipment leases. He was on the staff of the SEC for about 8 years, where he was involved with corporate reorganization cases and also served as an assistant general counsel. In private practice, he was appointed the receiver in connection with an SEC injunction action against David Peter Bloom, a Ponzi scheme case involving investor cash losses of about $13 million. Additionally, he has been a trustee in 10 other SIPC cases beginning in 1984, although these cases were much smaller than the Madoff case, which is, by some measures, SIPC's largest case ever.[18] He has served as trustee's counsel in two other cases. For his first case as trustee, Mr. Picard said SIPC contacted him and asked whether he would take the position. Subsequently, Mr. Picard said he has indicated to SIPC his continuing interest over the years in serving as a trustee, but did not solicit particular cases. Table 1 summarizes the Trustee's previous SIPC cases.

[17]SIPC senior management estimated that in SIPC's 290 liquidations, 186 individuals (excluding SIPC) have served as trustee or co-trustee, and at least 173 law firms have served as trustee's counsel. They also said that when the opportunity arises, SIPC designates firms new to SIPA cases.

[18]For example, according to SIPC senior management, the Madoff matter is SIPC's largest case as measured by missing assets and misstatement of customer assets, but is not the largest by number of customers or size of bankruptcy filing.

Table 1: The Trustee's Experience in Previous SIPA Cases, from 1984 through 2005

	Year	Number of customers	Customer distributions	Cause of firm's failure	Court-approved costs for trustee	Court-approved costs for trustee's counsel
Experience as SIPA trustee						
Jay W. Kaufmann & Company	1984	1,019	$3,134,917	Financial distress	$171,579	$128,903
Norbay Securities, Inc.	1986	9,103	16,531,987	Financial distress	256,555	88,139
Investors Center Inc.	1989	700	2,462,389	Financial distress, failure to comply with regulatory standards	516,586	245,263
Faitos & Co., Inc.	1991	39	1,361,543	Misappropriation	150,959	39,000
U.S. Equity Management Corp.	1995	15	996,345	Diversion	129,676	37,039
Hanover, Sterling & Co., Ltd.	1996	151	2,167,974	Unauthorized trading	349,716	300,627
Euro-Atlantic Securities, Inc.	1998	68	2,130,527	Unauthorized trading	348,963	212,877
Klein Maus & Shire, Inc.	2000	22	2,739,099	Unauthorized trading	278,195	275,460
Montrose Capital Management Ltd.	2001	10	917,146	Unauthorized trading	239,716	122,666
Park South Securities, LLC	2003	22	8,013,121	Conversion and unauthorized trading	1,077,996	2,843,040
Experience as trustee's counsel						
John Franklin & Associates, Inc.	1986	3	980,568	Misappropriation	—	23,265
Austin Securities, Inc.	2005	20	4,041,583	Unauthorized trading	—	98,855

Source: SIPC.

Notes: In each case, the trustee was a member of the trustee's counsel firm. "Conversion" is generally the wrongful possession or disposition of another's property as if it were one's own. "Diversion" is generally the unauthorized use of funds.

According to the Trustee, his involvement in the Madoff case began when he received a call from SIPC on December 11, 2008, the day Madoff was arrested, asking him to serve as trustee. On December 15, 2008, the U.S. District Court for the Southern District of New York appointed Mr. Picard as trustee, and his new law firm, Baker Hostetler, as trustee's counsel.[19] Selection of trustee's counsel was not an independent decision; both SIPC and the Trustee understood that trustee's counsel would be the

---

[19]As part of the appointment order, the case was removed to the U.S. Bankruptcy Court for the Southern District of New York.

Trustee's law firm. SIPC designated the Trustee's law firm as trustee's counsel, and the court issued an order to that effect.

Immediately before being formally appointed trustee, Mr. Picard changed law firms, joining Baker Hostetler on December 15, 2008. The Trustee told us that he had been on a year-to-year contract with his previous firm, and in the fall of 2008, with the end of his contract approaching and having received no indication it would be renewed, had begun to search for new employment. He told us that he explored employment with restructuring firms and other law firms, including Baker Hostetler, and also considered short-term contract work. After SIPC asked him to become the Madoff trustee on December 11, 2008, he said he felt he needed to make a decision on joining a firm quickly, in advance of his formal appointment, so that he would not be in the position of being at one firm and then potentially departing only a short time later in connection with the trustee work. Two firms with which he was in discussions were not able to come up with offers, the Trustee told us, but Baker Hostetler did so. In discussions with Baker Hostetler over the weekend of December 13-14, the Trustee said he did not bring up the subject of whether he was going to be appointed the trustee in the Madoff case, although he said his pending selection was known. According to the Trustee, Baker Hostetler representatives told him that the firm wanted him to join regardless of whether he would become the Madoff trustee. The Trustee noted that having Baker Hostetler as trustee's counsel is helpful because the firm has significantly more lawyers than his former firm, which makes the case easier to manage. He also has been able to rely on the in-house expertise of other partners who have assisted him in areas including management of remaining Madoff employees when he took on the case; real estate leases; intellectual property the Madoff firm owned; sale of Madoff assets, such as the market-making and trading side of the firm; and tax issues.

The Trustee also told us that a potential conflict at his former firm would have had to be resolved for him to serve as Madoff trustee had he remained there. He said that a partner at his former firm was going to provide representation in a Madoff-related matter, which could have presented a conflict. But the Trustee told us—and the SIPC President concurred—that had he accepted the trusteeship while at his former firm, arrangements would have been made to eliminate the conflict, so that the firm would not represent the other client. As a result, the Trustee said that any potential conflict was unrelated to his move between firms. The Trustee said he never asked SIPC for advice on what firm to join, nor did SIPC offer any guidance.

According to the Trustee, his compensation at Baker Hostetler is based on his overall contributions to the firm, as with other partners, and is not directly related to activity of the Madoff liquidation. He also noted he attracts other business to the firm in addition to the Madoff matter. The Trustee said he pays all court-awarded compensation he receives from the case as trustee to Baker Hostetler. He also noted that he is a contract partner, not an equity partner, at Baker Hostetler, meaning he does not have an ownership interest in the firm. The Trustee declined to provide us with details of his employment contract, saying Baker Hostetler's practice is for "closed" compensation contracts, where details are not known among members of the firm, but rather only by firm management. He said, however, that with his compensation based on his overall contributions, there are no provisions directly tied to the Madoff case, and his compensation does not vary specifically based on the results of Madoff case developments. He also noted that as trustee, his compensation is not on a commission basis, as provided in the Bankruptcy Code.[20]

SIPC and SEC Have Supported, and Courts Have Affirmed, the Trustee's Use of the Net Investment Method

In valuing customer claims filed as part of the Madoff liquidation, the Trustee selected NIM, which determines the amounts that customers are owed as the amounts they invested less amounts withdrawn. The Trustee, supported at the outset of the case by SIPC and, after nearly a year of analysis, by SEC as well, decided against valuing claims based on amounts shown on customers' final statements. The parties said this was on the grounds that it met statutory requirements, and that using statement amounts would effectively sanction the Madoff fraud by establishing claims according to the fictitious profits Madoff reported. NIM has consistently been used in SIPC liquidations involving Ponzi schemes, and the two courts that have considered the net equity issue in the Madoff case—the bankruptcy court and the U.S. Court of Appeals for the Second

---

[20]Section 326(a) of the Bankruptcy Code provides that in a case under chapter 7 or chapter 11, the court "may allow reasonable compensation...of the trustee for the trustee's services, payable after the trustee renders such services, not to exceed 25 percent on the first $5,000 or less, 10 percent on any amount in excess of $5,000 but not in excess of $50,000, 5 percent on any amount in excess of $50,000 but not in excess of $1,000,000, and reasonable compensation not to exceed 3 percent of such moneys in excess of $1,000,000, upon all moneys disbursed or turned over in the case by the trustee to parties in interest, excluding the debtor, but including holders of secured claims."

Circuit—have affirmed the Trustee's decision on this method for determining customer claims.[21]

The Trustee Decided to Use Method Typically Used in Ponzi Scheme Cases

In a SIPA liquidation, it is the trustee that decides on the method for determining customer claims. SIPA refers to this as calculating a customer's "net equity," and the statute generally provides that this amount is what would have been owed to the customer if the broker-dealer had liquidated all their "securities positions," less any obligations of the customer to the firm.[22] The statute also provides that the trustee shall make payments to customers "insofar as such obligations are ascertainable from the books and records of the debtor or are otherwise established to the satisfaction of the trustee."[23]

In SIPA liquidations not involving fraud, trustees typically determine that the amounts owed to customers match the amounts shown on their final statements—that is, the "final statement method" (FSM). In particular, according to SEC officials, in most SIPA liquidations, the books and records of the broker-dealer match the amounts shown on customers' final statements. In many cases in which a broker-dealer fails, customer accounts are transferred to another broker-dealer firm.[24] However, in cases involving fraud, amounts in customer accounts may not correspond to statement amounts—as in the Madoff case—and SIPA does not have any particular provisions for fraud cases beyond its general terms.

The Trustee told us that soon after the case began, and once he realized the investment advisory unit of the Madoff firm was a Ponzi scheme, he concluded that NIM—also known as "money-in/money-out"—was appropriate. As noted earlier, this method determines customer net equity

---

[21]Petitions seeking review of the case have been filed with the U.S. Supreme Court.

[22]15 U.S.C. § 78lll(11).

[23]15 U.S.C. § 78fff-2(b).

[24]SEC officials told us that whenever feasible, customer accounts are quickly transferred to another operating broker-dealer, to facilitate customers' orderly receipt of cash and securities, and to provide continuing access to brokerage services. In general, if the accounts and records are in order, a trustee likely can transfer the accounts to another broker-dealer in a process known as a bulk transfer. After such a transfer, customers have full access to their accounts. If a bulk transfer is not possible, the trustee returns customer securities and cash directly to customers on a pro rata basis through a claims process.

as customer deposits less customer withdrawals; it does not rely upon holdings reported on customers' final statements. Under NIM, Madoff claimants are divided into two categories: "net winners," who have withdrawn more than the amount they invested with the Madoff firm, and "net losers," who have withdrawn less than they invested. Following the firm's closure, the Trustee received 16,519 claims and denied most of them, chiefly because customers did not have accounts with the Madoff firm.[25] The Trustee said the firm had 4,905 active accounts at the time of closure. Determination of claim amounts under NIM resulted in 2,356 net loser accounts and 2,459 net winner accounts.

According to the Trustee, the chief reason for rejecting FSM in favor of NIM was that adopting customer statement amounts as the basis for account values would legitimize Madoff's fraud and cause account values to hinge on the fictitious trading and returns that Madoff reported to investors. The Trustee took the position that customer statements did not show "securities positions" that could be used for the net equity determination, because the statements were fictitious. Instead, the only Madoff records that reflected reality were those detailing the cash deposits and withdrawals of customers. Thus, the Trustee asserted that he was required to determine net equity based on these records, because they provided the only obligations that could be ascertained and established from the firm's books and records.

The Trustee also said that NIM was the most equitable method for Madoff customers. According to the Trustee, using FSM would allow some customers to retain fictitious "profits" they had withdrawn that actually were misappropriated investments of other customers. Moreover, FSM would divert the limited customer assets available from the liquidation by paying these fictitious profits at the expense of reimbursing real losses. The Trustee also said FSM could conflict with his obligation to recover through clawback actions fictitious profits that Madoff paid to some

---

[25]According to the Trustee, as of February 2012, customer claims in the case break down as follows:
  total claims received: 16,519;
  allowed claims: 2,426;
  denied claims: 2,703;
  other denied claims involving investors that held accounts at third parties: 10,976;
  withdrawn claims: 153; and
  other circumstances: 261.

investors.[26] If the Trustee were less able to make such recoveries, less money would be available to return to customers. The Trustee told us that he is not aware of any Ponzi case in which FSM was used to value customer claims.

We also found that the Trustee's selection of NIM was consistent with use of NIM in previous SIPA liquidations involving Ponzi schemes. According to SIPC data, among seven Ponzi scheme cases since 1995, including the Madoff case, all used NIM, in whole or in part, depending on facts and circumstances of individual accounts. (See table 2.)

Table 2: SIPA Liquidations Involving Ponzi Scheme Cases, from 1995 through 2012

Case	Year
Consolidated Investment Services, Inc.	1995
Old Naples Securities, Inc.	1996
New Times Securities Services, Inc., and New Age Financial Services, Inc.	2000
Donahue Securities, Inc., and S.G. Donahue Company, Inc.	2001
Northstar Securities, Inc.	2001
Continental Capital Securities, Inc.	2003
Bernard L. Madoff Investment Securities, LLC	2008

Source: SIPC.

Notes: SIPC told us that information on cases prior to 1995 was not readily available. The New Times case, which involved the use of NIM for some accounts and FSM for others, has been central to legal arguments on net equity determination in the Madoff case; see appendix III for details. Not included in the table is the 1997 Ponzi scheme case of First Interregional Equity Corporation. According to SIPC senior management, this was an atypical case that involved dual proceedings under SIPA and chapter 11 bankruptcy. The net equity of customers who were victims of the Ponzi scheme was never determined as part of the SIPC liquidation. Instead, customers were reimbursed from a settlement in the non-SIPA portion of the case.

Although the Trustee decided to use NIM to value Madoff customer claims, he also chose to recognize a portion of customer statement amounts—specifically, those dated before April 1, 1981. The Trustee told us this decision was due to gaps in available Madoff or third party records prior to that date, and that beginning with April 1, 1981, more complete

---

[26]SEC officials told us that clawbacks usually have not occurred in other Ponzi cases because the duration of the frauds was generally shorter, which limits the amount of time that customers had to make withdrawals that could be subject to recovery actions. SIPC senior management told us SIPA and the Bankruptcy Code authorize clawbacks, and that such actions have been brought where Ponzi schemes were involved.

and reliable records became available. The Trustee said he chose to recognize these older customer statement amounts in an attempt to favor customer interests, even though the amounts likely reflect some fictitious profits. The impact of this decision, however, is relatively minor, according to the Trustee—recognizing about $165 million in 371 accounts, equal to about 1 percent of total claims allowed and about 15 percent of total accounts with approved claims.

Questions have been raised whether the effect on the SIPC fund influenced selection of the net equity method, as acceptance of higher customer claims under FSM could have affected SIPC's liability under the coverage it provides to investors. However, the Trustee told us that effect on the SIPC fund did not enter into his selection, and that he did not discuss how the use of NIM would affect the fund with either SIPC or SEC.

SIPC and SEC Both Supported Use of NIM, Although SEC Considered Alternatives

Like the Trustee, SIPC quickly concluded that NIM was the appropriate method for determining customer claims, because of the fraud in the case and because using FSM would effectively sanction Madoff's activities. According to SIPC senior management, the focus in a net equity determination is on individual customer transactions—that is, officials do not consider at the case level which method might be best. In the Madoff case, the transactions were alike—fictitious. As a result, applying a single method of determining net equity to the entire Madoff case was appropriate.[27] Furthermore, while trading and reported investment profits were fictitious, records were available on individual customer deposits and withdrawals. Such records make NIM calculations possible, according to SIPC. SIPC senior management emphasized that final customer account statements are not the only "books and records" of the failed firm, as cited in the statute.[28]

---

[27]SIPC senior management told us that with the exception of some transactions believed to be executed on behalf of insiders to the scheme, all purported customer transactions were fictional. SIPC senior management also stated that Madoff reviewed securities trading data after the fact, selecting securities that had experienced good results. He then issued purported purchase and sales confirmations based on the already known favorable results. According to SIPC senior management, other than activity involving the insiders, there has been no indication that any trades claimed on customers' behalf were legitimate.

[28]15 U.S.C. § 78fff-2(b).

SIPC senior management told us that when the Madoff case began, they quickly began discussions aimed at producing agreement among SIPC, the Trustee, and SEC on the method for determining net equity. According to SIPC, such agreement was important in order to avoid a situation that had arisen in a previous case in which SEC took a position in court at odds with SIPC. Further, SIPC senior management said they wanted to reach consensus early in the liquidation out of concern that SEC would come under pressure to change its position as the extent of customer losses became clearer.

By February 2009, SIPC senior management believed that based on their discussions, they had achieved consensus with SEC on use of NIM. These discussions included a meeting with the SEC Chairman, who, according to SIPC, reported that a majority of commissioners supported NIM. SIPC senior management noted that NIM has unpleasant consequences in some cases, but that honoring final statements would mean others would receive less than the amount of their own contributions. Further, adopting FSM would have put at risk a large majority of asset recoveries the Trustee has secured, SIPC senior management told us, because some funds withdrawn by customers that otherwise could be subject to recovery actions under NIM would instead be recognized as legitimate under FSM and thus not subject to recovery.

Although initially agreeing on use of NIM, SEC staff continued to research other options in a process that would extend until November 2009. SEC officials told us their preliminary view in the early days of the case was that NIM appeared to be the only feasible alternative, because it was the most consistent with the statute and fraud law related to Ponzi schemes. However, they said there was no official SEC position at the time. SEC's continued examination was of great concern to SIPC, according to SIPC senior management, who told us they saw the continuing analysis as a reversal of the earlier support for NIM. SIPC also said that SEC's continuing analysis raised concerns because SIPC needed certainty on method for valuing claims in order to begin processing and paying them.

SEC officials told us they agreed it was important to settle on a method as quickly as possible, but that early in the case, a considerable amount of research remained necessary to formulate a recommendation for the commission's consideration. They said SEC's task was not to simply review SIPC's determination, but rather to examine the issue independently. With SIPC under considerable pressure to start making payments to Madoff customers, SEC's position was that the Trustee had to do what he thought was correct. If SEC came to a different view later, and the Trustee or the bankruptcy court determined changes needed to be made, claims payments would have to be adjusted as necessary.[29]

In a SIPA liquidation, SEC seeks to provide the maximum recovery possible under the law for former customers, according to SEC officials. Toward that end, in addition to NIM and FSM, SEC staff considered several net equity methods as part of their review:

- NIM plus an adjustment based on Treasury notes. The adjustment would apply an interest rate based on the yield of 13-week Treasury notes for periods in which Madoff customer statements indicated customer holdings were not in securities.[30]

- NIM plus an alternative adjustment based on Treasury notes. Under this alternative, the adjustment would be made on the assumption customers had been fully invested in 13-week Treasury notes for the life of their account. This revision was in recognition that positions reported on Madoff statements were fabricated.

- A combination of FSM and NIM, under which FSM would be used to pay claims against the SIPC fund up to the maximum protection of $500,000, and NIM would be used for claims against assets recovered by the trustee.

- NIM plus an adjustment for inflation (described more fully later in this report).

During their review, SEC officials met with outside parties who advocated for FSM.[31] These outside parties advanced arguments including that the Trustee's view of net equity was at odds with the statute and its legislative

---

[29]Within SEC, analysis of the net equity issue took place in three divisions: Trading and Markets, which oversees SIPC; the Office of General Counsel (OGC), which is responsible for SEC's legal positions; and Risk, Strategy, and Financial Innovation, which evaluated possible outcomes under different scenarios. The three divisions worked collaboratively on the issue, SEC officials told us, but ultimately, OGC came to drive the discussions, because it would be OGC that would present the agency's legal position.

[30]SIPC rejected this approach, telling us that customer statements were equally as fictitious whether they represented that holdings were in securities or other instruments such as cash. Internal SEC correspondence we reviewed raised a similar concern.

[31]SEC officials told us they did not document the number of meetings and who attended.

history and purpose. In a letter to SEC, several law firms noted that the typical Madoff customer received written trade confirmations and monthly statements, which they said are the basis for determining net equity under the statute. Further, they said the legislative history shows that Congress intended customers to have valid net equity claims even when securities reflected on their confirmations and account statements were never purchased. The outside parties also argued that the Trustee's position would erode investor confidence at a time—during the financial crisis— when markets and the securities industry could least afford it. They asked that SEC attempt to persuade the Trustee to reverse course, or if that was unsuccessful, seek a court order to that effect.

SEC officials characterized the meetings as an opportunity to listen and ask questions. They said they did not make any decisions based solely on information presented in these meetings, and that in general, the outside interests did not advance any new arguments. The clients of the law firms were undisclosed, but according to SIPC senior management, the parties represented were Madoff customers subject to large clawback actions. The SEC Inspector General told us that he does not believe there were any improper motivations in the lobbying by the outside groups, but that such meetings can create appearance problems because other parties, perhaps those with fewer resources and which SEC did not hear, might have had a different position. SEC officials told us they were open to meeting with any parties and did not turn down any requests to meet during this time.

Over the course of 2009, SEC staff conducted various analyses of past cases and alternative approaches for valuing customer claims. After receiving various memorandums and briefings, SEC commissioners voted in November 2009 to approve the staff's request to submit a brief to the bankruptcy court supporting the Trustee's use of NIM. As one commissioner said at the time, given the difficult situation it faced, the commission did all that it could do legally and equitably in opting for NIM.

Both SIPC senior management and SEC officials agreed with the Trustee that the effect on the SIPC fund played no role in the selection of NIM. Both said their approach was to make their best determination under the statute, without regard to cost. They told us they considered any impact on the fund only to identify what actions would be necessary for SEC to extend a loan to SIPC, to be funded by SEC borrowing from Treasury, should that be necessary to supplement fund balances to honor coverage commitments.[32] Further, even if FSM had been selected, the SIPC fund would not have become insolvent, SIPC senior management told us. Under FSM, based on the SIPC coverage limit of $500,000 per customer, the SIPC fund's maximum exposure would have been $2.1 billion, compared to an expected $889 million outlay under NIM.[33]

The use of NIM, rather than relying on final statement amounts, makes determination of customer net equity a more expensive process, SIPC senior management and SEC officials told us. But as with impact on the SIPC fund, they said that cost does not factor into selection of method. Instead, SIPC senior management told us, the higher expenses are necessary, because of the investigation required after Madoff's statements to customers were found to be fabricated. In any case, use of FSM would not have avoided substantial administrative costs, according to SIPC senior management. Such costs would still have totaled several hundred million dollars, they said, to conduct the liquidation, pursue recovery actions, and process claims.

Courts Have Affirmed the Trustee's Use of NIM

After the Trustee chose NIM and began to settle claims based on the net investments that Madoff customers had made to their accounts, a number of customers objected to this approach. As a result, the Trustee petitioned the bankruptcy court in August 2009 for proceedings to affirm his choice of NIM. Opposing claimants argued that the Trustee must use FSM because Madoff statements reflected securities positions that they had every reason

---

[32]An SEC Office of Inspector General report addressing portions of the Madoff case included comments from SEC personnel suggesting impact on the SIPC fund was a matter of concern to SIPC senior management in consideration of what net equity method should be used. See SEC Office of Inspector General, *Investigation of Conflict of Interest Arising from Former General Counsel's Participation in Madoff-Related Matters*, OIG-560 (Washington, D.C.: Sept. 16, 2011). SIPC senior management noted to us that these comments were second-hand, and reiterated that impact on the fund played no role in their consideration.

[33]SIPC senior management also told us that the burden customers might bear in pursuing a claim, such as financial costs, time investment, or other hardship, did not enter into the net equity decision. The main reason is that no matter what net equity method is used, it remains necessary to investigate the facts and evidence supporting claims. In any case, they said, trustee efforts to investigate claims can actually lessen the burden for customers. SIPC senior management said the Trustee spends considerable time reconstructing events and transactions on behalf of customers, and in the Madoff case, the Trustee is better positioned to do so than customers.

to believe were accurate and upon which they had relied. They emphasized SIPA's purpose of reinforcing investor confidence and cited the act's legislative history as indicating that securities positions set forth in broker-dealer statements need not be accurate to be covered under SIPA.

The opposing claimants further argued that Madoff's profits, while fictitious, may have been received and spent years ago, that customers paid taxes on them, and may have foregone other investment opportunities in reliance on investment results shown in their statements. They further maintained that, at least in the case of advances from the SIPC fund, use of FSM would not limit payments to reimburse net losers for their losses. This was because they viewed the SIPC fund as a source for paying customer claims that operated independently of any customer assets recovered by the Trustee. Thus, they claimed all customers, both net winners and losers, could receive up to $500,000 from the SIPC fund without affecting customer assets recovered during the liquidation.

Both sides contended that precedent dealing with SIPA liquidations involving Ponzi schemes supported their calculation method. In March 2010, the bankruptcy court affirmed the Trustee's determination, agreeing with the Trustee, SIPC, and SEC on their key arguments.[34] The court agreed with the Trustee that net equity can be based on "securities positions" only to the extent that such positions are "ascertainable from the books and records of the debtor" or "otherwise established to the satisfaction of the trustee." The court further agreed that in a Ponzi scheme like Madoff's—in which no securities were ever ordered or acquired—that "securities positions" do not exist, and the trustee cannot pay claims based on the false premise that customer positions are what the account statements purported them to be. The court added that legitimate customer expectations based on false account statements "do not apply where they would give rise to an absurd result."[35] It said the Madoff customer statements "were bogus and reflected Madoff's fantasy world of trading activity, replete with fraud and devoid of any connection to market prices, volumes, or other realities."[36] Instead, the court said the only verifiable amounts evident from the Madoff firm's books and records are customer

---

[34] *In re Bernard L. Madoff Investment Securities LLC*, 424 B.R. 122 (Bankr. S.D.N.Y. 2010).

[35] *Id.* at 135.

[36] 424 B.R. at 129-130.

cash deposits and withdrawals. (For a fuller discussion of legal issues involving determination of net equity in the Madoff case, see appendix III.)

The court also found that fairness and "the need for practicality" favored NIM.[37] It concluded that payments from the SIPC fund were inextricably connected to payments from customer assets, rejecting the argument by FSM proponents to the contrary. Thus, use of FSM for SIPC advance payments would diminish the amount available for distribution from the customer asset fund. Because there are limited customer funds, any funds paid to reimburse fictitious profits would no longer be available to pay other claims.

The court also agreed with the Trustee that NIM was more compatible with efforts to recover assets. The court said that customer withdrawals made in furtherance of a Ponzi scheme, and specifically, withdrawals based on fictitious profits, can be subject to recovery actions. NIM harmonizes the definition of net equity with clawback actions, by similarly discrediting withdrawals based on fictitious profits, and unwinding, rather than legitimizing, the fraud. The court noted that FSM, by contrast, would base compensation to customers on the same withdrawals the trustee has the power to seek to recover.[38]

In August 2011, the Court of Appeals for the Second Circuit affirmed use of NIM as the appropriate method in the Madoff case.[39] The appeals court found that while SIPA does not prescribe a single method for determining net equity in all situations, the Trustee's use of NIM was the best proposed method given the statutory definition of net equity. The court noted that use of FSM would have the absurd effect of legitimizing the arbitrarily assigned paper profits that Madoff's fraud produced. The court emphasized that while FSM may be appropriate in typical situations, the nature of the Madoff Ponzi scheme, including "extraordinary facts" of the Madoff fraud, point toward use of NIM. The court rejected the claimants' characterization of SIPA as providing an "insurance guarantee" against

---

[37]424 B.R. at 141.

[38]*Id.* at 136.

[39]*In re Bernard L. Madoff Investment Securities LLC*, 654 F.3d 229 (2d Cir. 2011).

Madoff's fraud; rather, it said, SIPA does not clearly protect against all fraud committed by brokers, or insure investors against all losses.[40]

Customer Claims Would Increase Significantly under FSM Compared with NIM

According to information we reviewed, the differences in customer net equity under the two approaches is significant, because during the decades of his fraud, Madoff reported considerable investment gains to his investors. According to SIPC, customer claims allowed under NIM total about $17.3 billion, while under FSM, the total would be approximately $57.2 billion. Table 3 shows a comparison of claims, broken down by account size, under the as-adopted NIM and the as-proposed FSM.

Table 3: Number of Accounts and Value of Claims under NIM and FSM

Account size	Under NIM (adopted by Trustee)		Under FSM (advocated by some customers)	
	Accounts	Claims Value	Accounts	Claims value
Less than $1 million	1,204	$381.9 million	1,485	$670.9 million
1-2.9 million	626	1.1 billion	1,372	2.5 billion
3-4.9 million	198	754.6 million	569	2.2 billion
5-9.9 million	153	1 billion	529	3.7 billion
10 million or greater	138	14 billion	499	48.1 billion
Other	—	—	5	76.9 million
Total	**2,319**	**$17.3 billion**	**4,459**	**$57.2 billion**

Source: SIPC.

Note: Totals may not sum due to rounding.

As table 3 shows, the number of accounts that potentially would have allowable claims under FSM nearly doubles from the corresponding number under NIM. This is because FSM generally accepts customer statements as accurate representations of holdings, and thus even those customers that withdrew more than they invested—net winners—would also be entitled to have their claims approved. Total account value would more than triple. However, this does not necessarily mean that customers would recover their statement amounts under FSM. Rather, the amounts distributed to customers will depend on how much the Trustee can

---

[40]*Id.* at 239.

recover during the liquidation. If the amount recovered is less than the amount of allowed claims—as is currently expected—then customers receive payments based on their relative share of total claims. Thus, the significance of using different methods for calculating net equity is that the different methods can affect customers' relative shares of total claims. In turn, that affects the amount of money they ultimately receive.

Adjusting NIM for Inflation Could Increase the Size of Customer Claims and Remains an Outstanding Issue

Although SEC supported the Trustee's decision to use NIM, SEC's position differed from the Trustee's and SIPC's in one respect: When SEC commissioners voted to support NIM, they also said customer deposits and withdrawals should be adjusted for inflation. According to SEC staff, such adjustments would account for the length of time the Madoff firm held customer funds. This has become known as the "constant dollar approach."[41] To date, neither the bankruptcy court nor the appeals court has addressed the merits of the SEC position. SEC officials told us they see the constant dollar approach as a way to treat customers more fairly and equally.

SEC's consideration of the constant dollar approach arose from the agency review, as described earlier, of potential methods for calculating customer claims. SEC officials told us that after they rejected FSM and adjustments based on Treasury notes, study continued on whether another method consistent with SIPA would allow customers to recover more money. However, the focus of their efforts shifted from investments that Madoff claimed to have made but did not, and toward the time value of money, pegged to when customers made their investments, so that customers would be treated equivalently in real dollar terms. The concept was that this would recognize the long duration of the Madoff fraud.

Under the constant dollar approach, a customer's series of deposits and withdrawals over time would be adjusted for inflation and converted into dollar amounts that reflect current price levels. The simplest instance would be a single customer deposit made years ago that would be converted into current dollars based on price changes over the specified period. For example, according to the Consumer Price Index, the value of a $10,000 deposit made 20 years ago would be $16,156 in 2012 dollars. Calculations would become more involved with multiple deposits and withdrawals over

---

[41]See 424 B.R. at 125, n. 8.

time, but the basic reasoning of converting past transaction amounts into current dollars would be the same, according to SEC officials.

SEC officials told us their analysis indicated this approach could be consistent with case law. Although case law has not specifically recognized inflation adjustments, they said, it does provide support for the general notion of seeking to treat investors equally. Translating that concept to the Madoff case, SEC viewed inflation-adjustment as a way to treat customers equally over time, during which price inflation would occur. In a memorandum to commissioners, SEC's Office of General Counsel said that failing to do so would ignore the effects of inflation on innocent investors and treat early victims of the fraud inequitably compared with later investors.

SIPC senior management disagrees with SEC's analysis and conclusion, saying the statute provides no authority for inflation adjustment and that no such authority can be inferred or implied. According to SIPC, determination of net equity is a specified mathematical function, and the notion of adjusting net equity determinations for inflation is an SEC-created approach that the statute does not support.[42] SIPC senior management also noted that adjusting customer claims for inflation has never come up before in any other SIPC case, because the fraud in the Madoff case is atypical in having such a lengthy duration. While inflation calculations likely could be done, there would be large costs in doing so, given the scope of the case and the number of transactions. SIPC senior management further noted that if inflation-adjustment were permitted, the size of some claims would increase. Because the pool of funds to satisfy customer claims is fixed, larger payouts to some could depress payments to others, according to SIPC senior management. This could lead to litigation among customers because some net winners could become net

---

[42]In addition, according to SIPC senior management, recent amendments to SIPA show Congress had no intent to allow inflation adjustment for net equity. Following changes made by the Dodd-Frank Wall Street Reform and Consumer Protection Act in 2010, there is now an inflation-adjustment provision built into SIPC coverage—but not for net equity. Rather, it involves determination of the amount of the standard maximum cash advance amount in a SIPC case. SIPC advocated for this change, executives told us. However, they said, the key point is that this provision does not apply to net equity. When adopting the change, Congress had the ability to add provisions for inflation-adjustment of net equity, but did not do so, they said.

losers.[43] We reviewed one sample of an inflation-adjusted Madoff account that illustrated how claims could change significantly. It showed a beginning balance of $130,000 in 1992, followed by a series of 23 withdrawals totaling $145,900 made through 2008. Thus, the customer had withdrawn $15,900 more than initially invested, and under NIM, is a net winner whose claim would be denied. But after adjusting the sequence of transactions for inflation, based on specific timing and amounts, the customer would become a net loser—having withdrawn $29,829 less, in inflation-adjusted dollars, than originally contributed.

The Trustee told us he did not consider a constant dollar approach, as it is not in the statute or supported by case law. He concurred with SIPC that claim amounts could increase considerably. As an example, he said, if a 9 percent annual interest rate, as allowed under New York fraud law, were applied, claims could grow by tens of billions of dollars, from their currently approved $17.3 billion.[44]

Following disclosure of a conflict of interest by a former SEC official in February 2011, SEC has plans to reconsider its position on supporting adjusting customer accounts for inflation. With the filing of a clawback suit by the Trustee against SEC's former General Counsel, it became public that the former official and his brothers had inherited a Madoff account from their mother.[45] In a report on the matter, the SEC Inspector General recommended—and the SEC Chairman agreed—that the commission should reconsider the inflation-adjustment issue because of concerns about the former General Counsel's participation in SEC's decision-making process.

The involvement of the SEC general counsel's office in the net equity issue began in January 2009, before the former General Counsel took his position on February 23, 2009. Thus, while the former general counsel

---

[43]One limited SEC study of about 2,100 accounts showed that adjusting for inflation increased estimated payments for 1,033 accounts, or about half, while reducing estimated payments for 438 accounts.

[44]SEC officials noted the 9 percent rate cited by the Trustee is a statutory judgment rate, not a measure, such as the Consumer Price Index, contemplated as an inflation-adjustment rate under a constant dollar approach.

[45]See OIG-560. The Inspector General told us he found no evidence that the former General Counsel's actions on the net equity matter were motivated by trying to serve his own financial interests, or that he had become subject to a clawback action.

became involved in the review, he did not initiate it. The Inspector General recommended that commissioners revote to avoid any possible bias or taint. The SEC Chairman has directed commission staff to review whether commissioners should readopt the constant dollar approach.

Cost of the Madoff Liquidation Will Be the Largest to Date, with Efforts to Recover Assets Driving Costs

Through October 31, 2011, the Trustee reported spending of $451.8 million for liquidation activities, with final costs expected to exceed $1 billion through 2014. To date, the two largest components of these costs have been legal costs of the Trustee and trustee's counsel, and costs for consultants. Although the Madoff case is expected to be SIPC's most costly case to date, the ratio of total costs to customer distributions is lower than for some other SIPC cases.

Total Administrative Costs of the Liquidation Have Reached $452 Million and Are Expected to Exceed $1 Billion

Through October 31, 2011, the latest date for which information was available, total administrative costs of the Madoff liquidation—ranging from office expenses to professional services—reached approximately $452 million. As shown in figure 3, the two major components have been legal costs, chiefly for time spent by the Trustee and his counsel, and consultant costs, for work such as investigating fraudulent activities of the Madoff firm and analyzing customer accounts. Legal costs represent the largest expense, according to a series of interim reports the Trustee has filed with the bankruptcy court, plus other information we reviewed.

Figure 3: Total Costs of the Madoff Liquidation, by Type, as of October 31, 2011

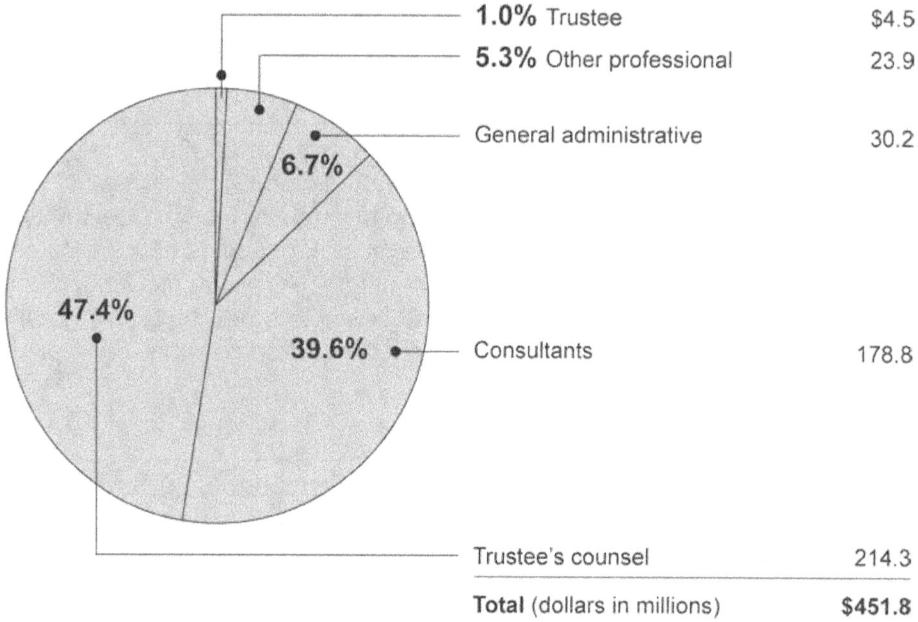

1.0% Trustee	$4.5
5.3% Other professional	23.9
General administrative	30.2
Consultants	178.8
Trustee's counsel	214.3
Total (dollars in millions)	**$451.8**

Pie chart segments: 1.0%, 5.3%, 6.7%, 47.4%, 39.6%

Source: GAO analysis of Trustee reports.

Note: General administrative category includes expenses such as computer, employee, insurance, office rent, utilities, taxes, and supplies.

The Trustee told us that total administrative costs are estimated to reach $1.094 billion through 2014.[46] The $1.094 billion for the Madoff case is approximately double the combined costs of $512.6 million for all 315 previously completed SIPC customer protection proceedings from 1971 through 2010, the latest year for which information was available.[47] Overall, a Ponzi scheme fraud is not necessarily intrinsically more expensive to handle, according to the Trustee. For instance, in the Madoff case, forensic analysis to determine what occurred at the firm has been similar to investigations in other Ponzi scheme cases. However, the Madoff case stands out for the

---

[46]Further increases are possible, depending on how liquidation proceedings develop, the Trustee said, and a new analysis will probably be done in the future.

[47]Costs in the bankruptcy of Lehman Brothers, Inc.—also a SIPC customer protection proceeding—are substantial as well. They total $498.1 million, according to the most recently available information. Unlike the Madoff case, the Lehman costs do not involve any advances by SIPC, and instead are being paid from debtor assets. The case is not yet complete.

duration of the fraud, its size, and the number of people involved, according to the Trustee, SEC officials, and SIPC senior management.

Trustee and Trustee's Counsel Costs

Although the Trustee directs the liquidation, the bulk of the costs of the liquidation are those associated with the legal work performed by attorneys of the law firm acting as the trustee's counsel. That firm, Baker Hostetler, performs work that includes assisting the Trustee's investigation; asset search and recovery, including related litigation; case administration; and document review. In addition to the Trustee's interim reports, periodic cost applications filed with the bankruptcy court for approval contain more detailed information on costs incurred by the Trustee and trustee's counsel. Our review of these cost applications, which cover from December 2008 through May 2011, found that costs for the Trustee and trustee's counsel were $230 million for this period (see table 4).[48]

Table 4: Approved Trustee-Related Legal Cost Requests, from December 2008 through May 2011

Dollars in millions

Cost category	Total
Trustee compensation	$4.9
Trustee's counsel compensation	220.2
Trustee's counsel expenses	4.9
Total	**$230**

Source: GAO analysis of Trustee and trustee's counsel cost applications.

[48]Because the interim reports and legal cost applications cover different periods, information contained in them does not correspond. Because the legal cost applications submitted for court consideration are more detailed, and because court approval is required for payment, our review of Trustee and trustee's counsel legal costs focused on the items submitted for court approval. In addition to the legal costs submitted by the Trustee and trustee's counsel, 19 other parties, mostly special counsel, have also submitted, and won approval of, additional costs totaling $25.3 million, or an amount equal to 11 percent of total Trustee and trustee's counsel costs approved. As of February 2012, the Trustee has retained, with the bankruptcy court's approval, 17 special counsel, consisting of 13 foreign law firms and 4 domestic law firms; this number has changed over time. Because our review focuses on the Trustee and trustee's counsel, we omit the other parties' costs from our discussion.

Notes: Totals may not sum due to rounding. The Trustee's expenses are minimal—a total of $2,500—and are not separately identified here. For the December 2008 to May 2011 period indicated, the Trustee and trustee's counsel have submitted seven cost applications, which the bankruptcy court has approved. In February 2012, the Trustee and trustee's counsel filed their eighth cost application, covering the period June 2011 to September 2011. The eighth application seeks approval for a combined total of approximately $48 million in compensation and $1.2 million in expenses, and as of the date of our report, the request was pending with the court. References in this report to the "latest" cost figures do not include amounts from the eighth application, and instead refer to court-approved costs through May 2011.

These costs reflect a substantial number of hours—597,052—that the Trustee and trustee's counsel have billed (see table 5). For the most recent reporting period, covering February to May 2011, about 100 partners, who are the most senior staff in the law firm, and 200 associate attorneys, worked on the case.[49]

Table 5: Total Hourly Billings for the Trustee and Trustee's Counsel, by Staff Category, from December 2008 through May 2011

Category	Hours billed
Trustee	6,704
Trustee's counsel partners	175,250
Trustee's counsel associate attorneys	335,191
Trustee's counsel nonlegal professional staff	79,907
Total	**597,052**

Source: GAO analysis of Trustee and trustee's counsel cost applications.

Our review of costs for the Trustee and trustee's counsel also identified several trends within the overall amounts.

Attempts to recover assets are driving costs. As shown earlier in table 4, the Trustee's costs alone are relatively small compared to the trustee's counsel costs. Within this larger category, costs for litigation to recover assets have risen sharply to account for a large majority of the trustee's counsel costs. As of December 2011, the Trustee told us about 1,050 lawsuits have been filed as part of efforts to recover assets on behalf of customers. These recovery actions are international in scope, with the Trustee reporting more than 70 actions involving foreign defendants. For example, actions have been filed in the United Kingdom, Bermuda, the

---

[49]The partner figure includes "of counsel" attorneys, who are nonpartner lawyers also participating in the case, such as on special assignment.

British Virgin Islands, Gibraltar, and the Cayman Islands. According to the Trustee, international investigations have involved identifying the location and movement of assets abroad, becoming involved in litigation brought by third parties in foreign courts, bringing actions before U.S. and foreign courts and government agencies, and hiring international counsel for assistance. As figure 4 shows, asset recovery actions—that is, avoidance or clawback actions—have outpaced all other trustee counsel costs as the case has progressed. According to SIPC senior management, the considerable expenses of the actions have been worthwhile, as the Trustee has produced $8.7 billion in recoveries for customers thus far.[50]

Figure 4: Trustee's Counsel Costs, by Category, from December 2008 through May 2011

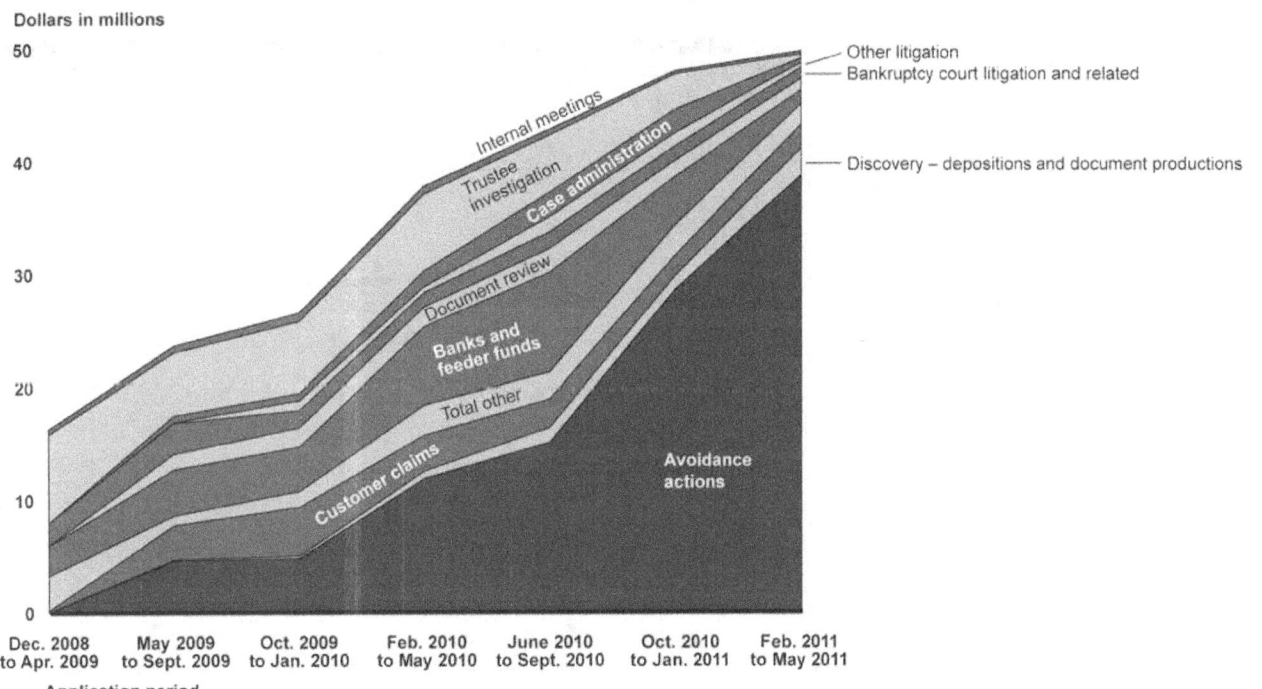

Source: GAO analysis of trustee's counsel cost applications

---

[50]In addition, as noted earlier, the Trustee in November 2011 reached a $326 million settlement with the Internal Revenue Service, to recover certain foreign withholding taxes paid on behalf of Madoff account holders, allegedly to make the Ponzi scheme appear authentic.

Partner hours have been declining. In general, billing rates for partners at the trustee's counsel firm are higher than rates for associate attorneys.[51] Thus, the more work partners handle, the higher the costs; while the more work that associates perform, the lower the costs. Our review showed that partner hours as a fraction of total hours claimed by the trustee's counsel have been declining steadily, from about 42 percent near the beginning of the case to about 28 percent in the most recent period (see fig. 5). The Trustee told us the partner hours have been declining as case activity has shifted. Through the end of 2010, as the Trustee and trustee's counsel were busy preparing to file the many complaints brought as part of the liquidation, partners were heavily involved in case preparation and policy decisions. Later, as cases moved into litigation, associate attorneys handled more of the load.

Figure 5: Partner Hours as a Percentage of Total Attorney Hours, from December 2008 through May 2011

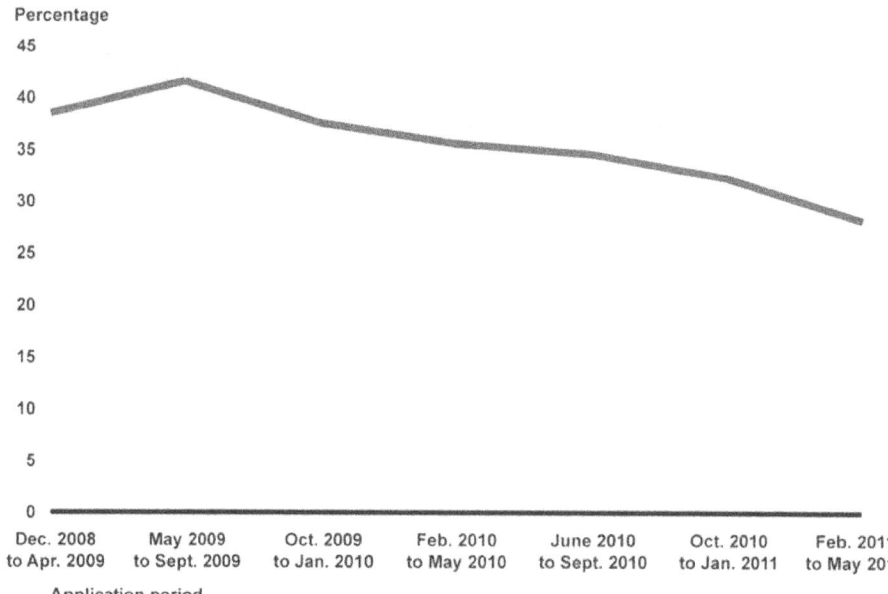

Source: GAO analysis of trustee's counsel cost applications.

---

[51]Comparing the billing rates of the trustees in the Madoff case and the Lehman Brothers, Inc., liquidation shows them to be roughly the same—$850 per hour for Madoff, and $891 for Lehman. A rate comparison alone, however, does not take into account how a firm's attorney resources are deployed in handling a case, which in turn influences total cost.

Higher-cost people have performed more work. Although the proportion of hours attributable to partners has been declining, we also found that within each category of professional work at the trustee's counsel—partners, associates, and nonlegal staff—higher-cost people have been performing a larger share of work. We examined the distribution of costs at two points during the Madoff liquidation: the second cost application following start-up of the case (covering May to September 2009), and the most recent cost application (covering February to May 2011). Figure 6 illustrates our findings, showing results for the partner category as an example. Partners whose billing rates are in the top 20 percent (the top quintile) of all billing rates for partners working on the Madoff case accounted for a greater share—about a third—of all partner hours compiled, and more than 40 percent of all partner billings in dollars. By contrast, partners whose billing rates are in the bottom 20 percent (the bottom quintile) accounted for a smaller share of activity—about 12 percent of hours compiled, and about 7 percent of all partner billings in dollars. Middle quintiles followed the same trend. We found that similar patterns applied for associate attorneys, and nonlegal staff such as paralegals, clerks, and librarians.[52] The Trustee attributed this trend to differences in billing rates among Baker Hostetler offices. Most case activity takes place in New York, where rates are higher than elsewhere. Attorneys in other offices, where rates are lower, provide assistance to New York-based lawyers, the Trustee said.

---

[52]We also examined whether individual attorneys' billing rates corresponded with experience levels but found considerable variance. As a result, we focused on billing rates, not years of experience.

Figure 6: Distribution of Partner Work, by Hourly Billing Rate Quintiles, from February 2011 through May 2011

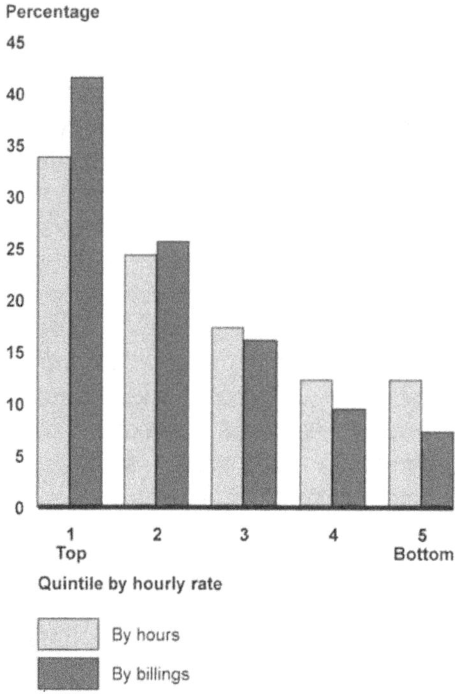

Percentage

Quintile by hourly rate

By hours
By billings

Source: GAO analysis of trustee's counsel cost applications.

Limited guidance is available to assess the reasonableness of legal costs, such as those incurred in the Madoff case. The American Bar Association (ABA) publishes "model rules," or recommended professional standards, including a model rule on professional conduct, which includes legal costs.[53] The rules are only advisory, but according to ABA, nearly every state patterns its professional conduct rules on the ABA model rule. According to ABA, there is no formula for determining whether costs charged in specific situations—or, in the case of the Madoff case, to hundreds of individual instances of litigation—are reasonable. Rather than provide a formula, the ABA model rule focuses on reasonability of legal costs and provides a number of qualitative factors that can be

---

[53]ABA is a voluntary professional association for the legal field, and provides law school accreditation, continuing legal education, information about the law, programs to assist lawyers and judges in their work, and initiatives to improve the legal system.

considered in evaluating reasonableness of attorney costs. Among the factors are the time and labor required; the novelty and difficulty of the questions involved; the skill needed to perform the legal service properly; and the experience, reputation, and ability of the lawyer(s) performing the services.[54]

Costs for Consultants

In addition to the costs for the Trustee and his counsel, there have been a number of other professional costs in the Madoff case. Largest among them, according to the Trustee, have been $178.2 million in consultant costs.[55] These costs include, for example, forensic accounting services performed as part of the fraud investigation. While legal costs have been increasing, consultant costs have been decreasing, reflecting their prominence earlier in the case (table 6).

Table 6: Consultant Costs, May 2009 through September 2011

Period ending	Consultant costs (in millions)
May 31, 2009	$14.6
October 31, 2009	34.3
February 28, 2010	19.1
September 30, 2010	54.9
March 31, 2011	29.6
September 30, 2011	25.7
Total	**$178.2**

Source: GAO analysis of Trustee's interim reports.

Note: We also obtained information for the single month of October 2011, which totaled $661,671.

Total Costs of the Madoff Liquidation Have Been Within SIPC's Range of Experience

While the total costs of the Madoff liquidation are expected to be higher than all other completed SIPC cases combined, we found that costs as estimated thus far, as a percentage of current recoveries for customers, have been within the range experienced in past SIPC cases. Specifically, we examined SIPC-reported total costs as a percentage of distributions to

---

[54]Other factors from ABA's nonexhaustive list are the likelihood, if apparent to the client, that the acceptance of the particular employment will preclude other employment by the lawyer; the fee customarily charged in the locality for similar legal services; the amount involved and the results obtained; time limitations imposed by the client or by the circumstances; and nature and length of the professional relationship with the client.

[55]Other types, for example, include investment banker fees and SEC receiver expenses.

customers in completed SIPC cases.[56] We grouped these cases on an annual basis, focusing on years in which there were at least $50 million in distributions.[57] As shown in figure 7, the currently estimated total costs of the Madoff liquidation, as a percentage of current recoveries, are within the range of costs incurred in previous SIPC cases. For individual years, the cost percentages have ranged from a low of 0.3 percent (2001) to a high of nearly 40 percent (1990, when there were considerable expenses in one relatively large case[58]). For the Madoff case—which is not yet complete, and as discussed earlier, is atypical—the cost percentage is currently 11 percent, based on the latest estimate of total cost ($1.094 billion), and $8.7 billion in current recoveries from the Trustee's efforts, the $326 million Internal Revenue Service (IRS) settlement, plus an expected $888.5 million in SIPC customer advances. The ratio for the Madoff case could change, depending on future costs incurred and if the Trustee secures additional recoveries.

---

[56]For our analysis, we defined total costs as administrative cost distributions from the estate plus SIPC advances for administrative costs. We defined customer distributions as those from the estate plus SIPC advances for securities and cash.

[57]We also excluded cases prior to and including 1978 because according to SIPC, the method for covering administrative costs changed with SIPA amendments that year. Before the amendments, administrative costs could be paid from customer funds.

[58]This 1990 case was the liquidation of Blinder, Robinson & Co., Inc., a Colorado "penny stock," or low price, firm. According to SIPC, no other brokerage firm would accept a transfer of this firm's customer accounts because they contained essentially worthless securities that had been sold to dissatisfied customers, As a result, customer claims had to be determined on a position-by-position basis, which was expensive.

Figure 7: Total Costs as Percentage of Customer Recoveries for Madoff and Completed SIPC Cases, for Selected Years from 1979 to 2010, Ranked by Cost Percentage

	Percentage	Customer distributions
2001	0.3%	$11,845,935,313
1987	3.4	197,792,815
2010	5.6	890,560,975
1997	8.1	623,146,465
1983	8.6	207,094,604
1984	9.5	124,408,758
1988	9.7	134,911,794
1999	9.9	443,052,428
1985	10.4	502,269,758
Madoff	11.0	9,914,545,672
1981	14.3	314,991,183
2003	14.5	77,111,217
1986	15.1	51,283,635
1990	38.4	103,794,397
Total	(All years shown) 2.5%	$15,516,353,342
	(Excluding 2001) 9.5%	$3,670,418,029

Source: GAO analysis of SIPC, Trustee information.

Notes: Total cost figures do not include the Madoff case. Customer distributions for the Madoff case are not complete; figure is based on current recoveries by the Trustee, the IRS settlement, and advances from SIPC.

The 13 years shown in figure 7 cover 104 cases that together account for $15.5 billion in customer distributions.[59] Total costs for all these cases equal 2.5 percent of customer distributions. We note, however, that results for one year—2001—reflect almost entirely the outcome of a single large case, in which a firm failed but recoveries were sufficient to

---

[59]The $15.5 billion figure for the selected years is 99.1 percent of all distributions for the entire 1979 to 2010 period, according to our analysis of SIPC information.

reimburse all valid customer claims fully. Excluding 2001, total costs for all cases as a percentage of customer distributions are equal to 9.5 percent.[60]

Various Steps Are Being Taken to Control Madoff Liquidation Costs

In a SIPA liquidation, each of the main parties—the trustee, SIPC, the bankruptcy court, and SEC—has a role in examining costs. These roles vary by the party and the stage of the proceeding.

Trustee Efforts to Control Costs

The Trustee noted that while he previously was at SEC and when serving as U.S. trustee, he had experience reviewing fee applications. He described a variety of ways by which he seeks to hold down expenses of the Madoff liquidation. The general process for approval of costs begins with the Trustee, who reviews them before submitting them to SIPC for its review, prior to submission to the bankruptcy court. For billings, the Trustee conducts a two-level review of Madoff-related time entries. Following completion of work, a mid-level attorney reviews the billings, and then a partner conducts another review. This second review is in tandem with SIPC, the Trustee told us. The purpose of these reviews is to determine whether too much time has been billed for a particular task. If so, it is written off, the Trustee said. Information the trustee's counsel produced for us, covering from inception through January 2011, showed about 1 percent of hours worked not being billed, with about another 1.5 percent of hours being written off after review. The Trustee also said that he does not bill for 5 percent to 10 percent of the time he spends on the case.

The Trustee said a similar review of billings takes place for costs submitted by other law firms and consultants that the Trustee and trustee's counsel use in their work. The Trustee said that in some cases, amounts claimed are reduced. However, the Trustee did not have specific amounts for any such reductions. The outside entities also discount their

---

[60]The single large case was MJK Clearing, Inc., a Minneapolis, Minnesota, brokerage firm with about 63,200 retail and 1,800 institutional customer accounts. MJK also cleared the accounts of other broker-dealers, making it responsible for about 175,000 customers. After the U.S. District Court ordered the firm's liquidation, the SIPA trustee arranged transfer of the customer accounts to another clearing firm, enabling customers to access their funds. The cause of the firm's failure involved defaults by a securities lending counterparty. With settlement of the litigation, the trustee was able to pay all creditors and return SIPC's advances, with interest. Total customer distributions, according to SIPC, were $11.8 billion, none of which were ultimately paid by SIPC.

billings at least 10 percent, as the Trustee and trustee's counsel do, with some providing 11 or 12 percent discounts.

In addition to billing reviews, the Trustee also described other approaches intended to help ensure that costs incurred are necessary and reasonable.

- *Teams.* Using teams, in which the same people work on similar matters, to help achieve greater consistency and efficiency. For example, the Trustee uses teams for different tasks, such as motions, discovery, and litigation. For litigation, for example, the trustee's counsel has set up about 16 teams, which work on similar topics, such as employee-related, review of charities, or family-related matters. The teams follow cases from beginning to end, taking advantage of experience gained through the process and limiting additional costs that could occur if staff were assigned work in unfamiliar areas, according to the Trustee.

- *Digitizing information.* Computerizing information as much as possible allows for faster, more efficient retrieval of information. This has involved significant up-front costs, but the Trustee noted that it reduces costs over time by avoiding the need to undertake time-consuming, expensive manual searches through thousands of boxes of paper material.[61]

- *Budgeting work in advance.* The Trustee said he uses a process in which consultants must fill out project forms and provide budgets, which are submitted and must be approved by trustee's counsel. SIPC also receives some of these budgets. When bills are received later, the trustee's counsel compares the amount claimed with the budget, and there have been instances in which costs exceeding budgeted amounts have been refused, according to the trustee.[62]

---

[61]The firm has also built in-house tools for managing discovery that help manage costs, but these are used for other clients as well, and not exclusively on the Madoff case. For example, documents have been computerized, with the ability to search documents by keyword.

[62]The Trustee and his counsel do not mark up costs submitted by vendors, consultants, or others, according to the Trustee. The Trustee reviews invoices, after which they are sent directly to SIPC for review and approval.

When the Trustee has completed in-house review of costs, he presents them to SIPC for review. The Trustee may hold informal discussions with SIPC before submitting actual costs for formal consideration. SIPC also may contact outside vendors directly to inquire about charges. SIPC does not pay for some charges, and following discussions with SIPC, the Trustee may decide to write off some costs, according to the Trustee.

SIPC Efforts to Control Costs

As SIPC senior management said is typical, at the outset of the case, they sought and obtained a 10 percent reduction in the hourly rates of the Trustee and trustee's counsel. According to our review, this 10 percent reduction has produced savings of $25 million through May 2011. In addition, the Trustee and trustee's counsel have provided additional reductions of $5.4 million over costs they said would customarily be billed.

Some have suggested that SIPC should have sought a discount greater than 10 percent. For example, the SEC Office of Inspector General has reported that an SEC bankruptcy attorney raised questions whether a 10 percent discount for SIPC cases is sufficient.[63] Similarly, the Inspector General noted to us that the Madoff case began during the recent financial crisis, when law firms' business was suffering, and suggested that as a result, SIPC would have had strong leverage to negotiate lower compensation for firms.

SIPC senior management, however, told us that a 10 percent reduction is appropriate for several reasons. Above that amount, service providers object, and a 15 percent discount is not economical for sophisticated work like that required in the Madoff case, according to SIPC senior management. Also, SIPC senior management noted that liquidation cases such as the Madoff matter draw highly qualified talent in opposing counsel, so that as a result, SIPC also must draw upon highly qualified providers. Furthermore, the 10 percent discount, coupled with "holdbacks"—in which payment of approved amounts is not released until later—amount to a significant burden on the service provider, according to SIPC. Finally, SIPC senior management said that the results the Trustee has produced to date support the costs incurred. For these reasons, SIPC has not sought a reduction greater than 10 percent in the Madoff case.

---

[63]See SEC Office of Inspector General, *SEC's Oversight of the Securities Investor Protection Corporation's Activities*, report no. 495 (Washington, D.C.: Mar. 30, 2011).

In addition to the 10 percent discount, SIPC has also created guidelines for review and approval of costs.[64] The guidelines cover matters including obtaining a fee discount; submitting costs; reviewing costs submitted; and documenting questions and discussions relating to the review of costs, including items flagged for attention or reduced or written off. Under these guidelines, a SIPC attorney reviews each time entry and expense item submitted, after which they prepare a memorandum to the SIPC general counsel, summarizing findings and making recommendations for approval. The general counsel is to review the memo and recommendations, before approving, modifying, or rejecting the cost request.[65] SIPC senior management told us they followed the guidelines in the Madoff case.[66] Also as part of this portion of the review process, SIPC's general counsel makes a line-by-line review of Trustee and trustee's counsel invoices, according to SIPC senior management.

Because costs in the Madoff case are so much greater than in previous SIPC cases, the Trustee, working with SIPC, has established "litigation budgets" for the many lawsuits resulting from the case.[67] These budgets detail expected costs of specific litigation, and for each case, divide tasks into specific categories, including research, drafting, motions, discovery, trial, appeal, and collection. According to SIPC senior management, this budgeting process is aimed at managing costs in advance or as they are

---

[64] *Securities Investor Protection Corporation Guidelines for Reviewing Applications and Monthly Invoices For Compensation and Reimbursement of Expenses Under Section 5(b)(5) of the Securities Investor Protection Act, 15 U.S.C. § 78eee(b)(5).* SIPC senior management told us these guidelines were likely created in the 1990s, and updated in 2003, but could not specify dates.

[65] The SEC Inspector General confirmed to us SIPC's close review of costs submitted in the Madoff case, saying his office's review showed all individual cost items were being examined.

[66] In particular, SIPC senior management told us, each month, SIPC's senior associate general counsel for dispute resolution, who is the principal SIPC attorney assigned to the Madoff case, closely reviews each cost record. The senior associate general counsel has been reviewing fees for SIPC for many years, the SIPC President told us, and his knowledge and experience are a key part of the process. To judge appropriateness of costs claimed, SIPC senior management told us the first step is that the person with the most knowledge of the case is the person who conducts the initial review. Issues examined include whether it appears too senior a lawyer worked on a task, whether too many hours were spent on a task, or whether too many people were involved with a task.

[67] According to SIPC senior management, litigation budgets have been used in some other SIPA cases since the 1990s. The use of such budgets is especially important in the Madoff case, they said, given the unprecedented scope of litigation stemming from it.

being incurred, rather than after-the-fact. In addition, several SIPC personnel are in daily contact with the Trustee or trustee's counsel. As a result, they are aware what activities are planned, and will discuss them ahead of time. They also discuss possible future actions. SIPC senior management told us the Trustee has revised certain planned actions or changed direction as a result of such discussions during the case.

We sought details on the extent to which SIPC has reduced or disallowed expenses submitted by the Trustee. SIPC senior management declined to provide documentation of its cost reviews, citing attorney work-product privilege. According to SIPC, releasing such information could provide an unfair advantage to litigation opponents and undermine attempts to recover assets on behalf of customers. Similarly, SIPC noted that releasing the litigation budgets could allow an opposing party to see how much has been allocated for an activity in litigation, which can provide a tactical advantage to opposing parties. However, the trustee's counsel provided us information on amounts written off at SIPC's request. According to this information, the trustee's counsel has written off, at SIPC's request, less than 1 percent of hours submitted. For the Trustee, SIPC-requested reductions to billings have been about 0.02 percent, according to the information provided by the trustee's counsel. SIPC senior management also declined to provide other cost review-related information we requested, again citing attorney work-product privilege.

The Bankruptcy Court's Role in Evaluating Legal Costs

In the Madoff case, the bankruptcy court has a limited ability to oversee costs. As noted earlier, the Trustee and trustee's counsel submit legal costs to SIPC, which reviews them, before filing with the bankruptcy court a recommendation on what the court should approve. SIPC files the recommendation after the trustee and trustee's counsel file their detailed cost applications with the court. Under SIPA, the court must approve cost applications if two conditions are met: (1) if there is no reasonable expectation of SIPC recouping its advances, and (2) if SIPC recommends to the court that it approve the costs requested by the trustee and trustee's counsel. In the Madoff case, both conditions have been met.

For the first condition, SIPC does not anticipate recouping its administrative advances because it expects that recoveries by the Trustee will be insufficient to cover all approved customer claims. SIPC senior management told us that they have opted to devote all asset recoveries—of both investor funds and sale of assets of the Madoff firm itself—to repaying approved customer claims. If a trustee can recover assets that exceed the amount of allowed customer claims, SIPC has a priority claim on the excess assets, in order to recoup its advances to cover liquidation costs. However, based on expected recoveries in the Madoff case, SIPC senior management does not expect there will be any excess assets. The current Trustee estimate of allowed claims is $17.3 billion, compared with $9.1 billion in Trustee recoveries and settlements. Thus, about $8.3 billion in additional recoveries would be needed, and based on current Trustee assets, lawsuits filed, and the estimated possibilities for recoveries arising from that litigation, SIPC senior management does not now expect this level of recoveries to occur.

For the second condition, SIPC has recommended that the bankruptcy court approve the legal costs requested in the applications submitted to the bankruptcy court. SIPC senior management told us that the statute requires the court to defer to SIPC's judgment on the appropriateness of expenses because it is SIPC that faces the economic risk of covering the costs in situations where SIPC does not expect recoveries to be sufficient to recoup its advances. For the first seven rounds of approved cost applications to date, the bankruptcy court has approved all of the legal compensation and expense requests submitted by SIPC for the Trustee and trustee's counsel. Although the court has been obliged to approve the cost applications because the two conditions have been met, the judge has said in hearings on the applications that notwithstanding the statutory requirement, he would nevertheless approve the costs on the basis of the work performed.

SEC Oversight of SIPC Liquidation Expenses

Although SEC has oversight authority over SIPC, it does not have a direct role in approving costs incurred in any particular SIPC liquidation. Instead, fee exams typically take place as part of its general examinations of SIPC, and SEC officials told us they plan a review of Trustee and trustee's counsel costs in coming months. In a March 2011 report, the SEC Inspector General noted that the Madoff and Lehman Brothers cases—the two largest liquidations in SIPC history—had focused new attention on concerns about the amount of trustee fees. The report made recommendations to improve SEC's oversight of SIPC liquidation costs. For example, the report recommended that SEC encourage SIPC to negotiate more vigorously with court-appointed trustees to obtain fee reductions greater than 10 percent and to develop a more regular process for monitoring SIPC's oversight of costs, rather than relying on examinations that do not occur regularly. The report also asked SEC to assess whether SIPA should be modified to allow bankruptcy judges presiding over SIPA liquidations to assess the reasonableness of administrative costs in cases in which SIPC pays the costs. The respective units of SEC indicated they concurred with these recommendations, and SEC officials told us that formal responses are being prepared.

SIPC, SEC, and the Bankruptcy Court Have Been Satisfied That the Trustee Has Made Sufficient Disclosures

Trustees for SIPA liquidations generally have the same duties as trustees for liquidations under chapter 7 of the Bankruptcy Code. Under this chapter, a trustee must make certain information disclosures, including:

- furnishing information about the estate and the estate's administration as requested by parties in interest, unless such disclosure is restricted by a court order;

- providing periodic reports and summaries of the operation of the bankrupt firm if it continues operating; and

- making a final report and filing a final account of the administration of the estate with the court and with the U.S. trustee.

SIPA directs a trustee to make the disclosures required under chapter 7 but also directs a trustee to include in such reports information on progress made in distributing cash and securities to customers. In addition, SIPA directs the trustee to promptly investigate the acts, conduct, property, liabilities, and financial condition of the firm being liquidated and report this information to the court. The trustee must also report to the court any facts learned by the trustee regarding fraud, misconduct, mismanagement, and irregularities, and any causes of action available to the estate as a result; and, as soon as practical, submit a statement of the investigation.

The Trustee Has Disclosed Information in Variety of Ways

Through a variety of means, the Trustee has made disclosures that address the statutory requirements. As of January 2012, the Trustee had issued six interim reports to the bankruptcy court that outline progress made in liquidating the Madoff firm. These interim reports have been filed approximately every 6 months.[68] The first report, filed in July 2009, gave the status of the Trustee's activities in administering the estate, his progress in addressing customer claims, and results to date from his investigation of the Madoff firm's activities. The report also included a

---

[68]These interim reports were filed on July 9, 2009; November 23, 2009; April 9, 2010 (amended Apr. 14, 2010); October 29, 2010; May 16, 2011; and November 15, 2011.

discussion of Madoff's fraudulent scheme, including his admitting to soliciting billions of dollars under false pretenses and failing to invest customer funds as promised. The Trustee said that extensive investigation of the firm's financial affairs inside and outside the United States revealed "a labyrinth of interrelated international funds, institutions, and entities of almost unparalleled complexity and (breadth)." The Trustee also noted that he was providing information to, and coordinating efforts with, other parties investigating the firm, including SEC, the Federal Bureau of Investigation, the U.S. Attorney's Office, and other regulators. The Trustee's other five interim reports provide information on similar issues, including the status of the investigations.

The Trustee has also provided various records to the court, as part of litigation involving his activities, which provide disclosures of the type required under the Bankruptcy Code and SIPA. For example, in a motion filed in October 2009 asking the bankruptcy court to affirm the use of NIM in determining customer claims, he included the report of a consultant hired to review the Madoff firm's activities in detail.[69] This report described, among other things, how little trading was done as part of the investment advisory business, and it also included statements from a Madoff firm employee who admitted to creating fake investment positions that were reported to customers on their statements.

The Trustee also has provided information to individual Madoff customers. To address customer claims, the Trustee told us that he provided determination letters to Madoff customers, showing individual account transactions and how net equity for their accounts was determined. For customers with questions about their claims determinations, the trustee's counsel was available to provide additional information, which in some cases, involved sharing information contained in the records maintained by the Madoff firm. The Trustee has also provided information to former Madoff account holders seeking information necessary for tax returns or for filing fraud claims under homeowner's insurance coverage. The Trustee told us he has not provided information about the fraud in general because individual customers do not need such information to have their claims processed.

---

[69]*Declaration of Joseph Looby in support of Trustee's Motion for an order upholding trustee's determination denying "customer" claims for amounts listed on last statement, affirming trustee's determination of net equity, and expunging those objections with respect to the determinations relating to net equity* (Oct. 16, 2009).

To facilitate access to customer records, the Trustee has created an "electronic data room." Initially, access was limited to customers sued by the Trustee that were determined to be net winners—those who withdrew more than they invested—and who were deemed to have acted in good faith without knowledge of the fraudulent nature of the firm's activities. In January 2012, the bankruptcy court judge granted a motion by the Trustee to expand access to the data room to attorneys for nongood faith defendants with whom the Trustee is in litigation.

In addition, the Trustee maintains a public website that contains a large volume of information about the case. It includes a timeline of the liquidation and provides data on the amount of customer assets recovered, amounts distributed to customers, and amounts committed by SIPC to date. The website also includes more than 600 selected court filings, which are provided in a searchable database with the original documents available for download. These documents date to the start of the Madoff liquidation in December 2008. All six interim reports filed by the Trustee, plus amendments, are included. In addition, the website provides information on the claims process, including links to SIPA, SIPC, and orders of the bankruptcy court. The website also has a page for the Trustee's hardship program, under which the Trustee does not seek to recover assets from customers suffering from particular financial or other hardships.[70]

Recently, expert reports produced as part of the Trustee's investigation have been made public, which the Trustee said contain extensive details on proof of fraud at the Madoff firm and its subsequent insolvency.

---

[70]Factors considered in making hardship program decisions include: advanced age; inability to pay for necessary living expenses, such as housing (including loss of home to foreclosure), food, utilities and transportation; inability to pay for necessary medical expenses; need to return to work after having previously retired (special consideration given to those who can no longer return to their former employment); declaring personal bankruptcy; and inability to pay for the care of dependents.

Although Some Have Sought Additional Trustee Disclosures, SIPC, SEC, and the Bankruptcy Court Say Information Released Has Been Sufficient

Although some parties have argued that the Trustee's disclosures have not met statutory requirements, SIPC and SEC officials told us they view the Trustee's disclosures to date as sufficient. SIPC senior management told us that early in the case, the Trustee did not release many details, to avoid tipping off potential civil and criminal defendants that would become target of legal actions. More recently, according to SIPC, as that concern eased, the Trustee has been doing an exemplary job in releasing information relevant to account holders and the public. SIPC senior management told us they expect the Trustee will file a complete report of his investigative activities after officials are satisfied that legal actions and investigations will not be endangered. While the Trustee has not yet issued such a report, complaints filed in the case provide a considerable amount of information that will eventually be released, they said. SEC officials also told us that while the statute provides no standards for the extent of disclosures that must be made, the Trustee has made considerable information available, which appears to be complete for the relevant topics.[71] The officials said some may not like decisions the Trustee has made, but there has been no lack of information about them.

An attorney representing former Madoff customers offered a different view to us, saying the Trustee has not provided information critically important for account holders making claims and those who are the subject of clawback actions by the Trustee. In particular, according to the attorney, while the Trustee has asserted that all reported trading activity was fictitious, and that the Madoff investment advisory arm operated independently from the rest of the Madoff firm, that cannot be established from information released thus far. The attorney told us he believed that more complete disclosure would show at least some legitimate trading activity on behalf of customers, which is important because investment returns from that activity would affect claims determination and what amounts the Trustee could seek to claw back.

In April 2010, attorneys representing various Madoff customers filed a motion with the bankruptcy court to compel additional disclosures by the Trustee, arguing that reports filed "discuss the nature of his investigation

---

[71]Under SIPA, the trustee reports "shall be in such form and detail as (SEC) determines by rule to present fairly the results of the liquidation proceeding as of the date of or for the period covered by such reports…." 15 U.S.C. § 78fff-1(c). SEC has not issued any such rules, but both SEC officials and SIPC senior management told us this has not been a significant issue.

in sweeping terms, with a bare minimum of detail and only conclusory statements about what has actually been uncovered." However, the Trustee told us he believes he has made great efforts to respond to the public, noting his interim reports, a recent redesign of the website, and his attempts to update case statistics at least every couple of weeks. By contrast, he said in a typical chapter 7 bankruptcy case, the only information available would be documents filed with the court. According to the Trustee, there is no information, other than litigation-related, that individual account holders might want but have not been able to get.

In his brief opposing the customers' motion to compel additional reporting, the Trustee said that in his many filings seeking recovery of customer assets, he has detailed the Madoff fraud and identified those he alleges were involved or knew of the fraud. He argued that the customers seeking additional disclosure were seeking to sidestep the Federal Rules of Civil Procedure and Bankruptcy Procedure that govern disclosure in litigation. These rules, covering what is known as the "discovery process," address matters such as parties making inquiries of each other and requests for the production of documents. As litigation proceeds, customers seeking greater disclosure will receive information through the discovery process and will have opportunity to access and challenge the Trustee's evidence, according to the Trustee. The attorney representing former Madoff customers, however, told us that while the discovery process will provide an opportunity for disclosure of some information, that process will be prohibitively expensive for many customers, and in any case, is not likely to develop case-wide information of value to all customers.

The bankruptcy judge denied the customers' motion to compel additional disclosures from the Trustee, calling the action a discovery dispute, rather than a failure by the Trustee to follow the statute. He said the Trustee has satisfied his disclosure obligations under SIPA and the Bankruptcy Code "by creating a thorough and specific record regarding Madoff's fraud." Affirming the Trustee's position, the judge said the demands will be satisfied during court-regulated discovery as litigation proceeds. The customers filed a motion for leave to appeal the bankruptcy court ruling, which the district court denied.

Conclusions

When a broker-dealer firm fails, and large sums of customer assets could be at risk, SIPC must move quickly to appoint a trustee and trustee's counsel in order to safeguard those assets and to maximize the possibility of any recoveries for customers. Toward that end, SIPC maintains an informally assembled roster of candidates, and its senior management confers before the SIPC president uses his professional judgment to select a trustee. In the Madoff fraud, SIPC moved to appoint a trustee and trustee's counsel within hours after Madoff was taken into custody.

Notwithstanding the need to move quickly, however, our review identified two areas in which SIPC's selection process could be improved. First, while SIPC seeks to identify potential trustees for its liquidations, it lacks a formal, documented outreach procedure for identifying those candidates. Although SIPC believes the field of broker-dealer bankruptcy is sufficiently small that the relevant parties are known, undertaking additional efforts to more systematically identify candidates would help ensure that the range of choices reflects the widest capabilities available in the most cost-effective fashion. Such outreach efforts could be tailored for SIPC's purposes, so that they are not excessively time-consuming or resource-intensive. Second, while SIPC draws on the experience and expertise of its senior management in selecting trustees, that process, including criteria for selection, is not documented or transparent. This lack of transparency can contribute to questions and concerns about SIPC's decisions. Better documentation of the selection process and criteria could help address some of these concerns.

Recommendations for Executive Action

To help ensure that the pool of providers that could be employed in SIPC liquidations is as broad as reasonably possible, and to improve the transparency of SIPC's selection of trustee and trustee's counsel for liquidations, the SEC Chairman should take the following two actions:

1. Advise SIPC to document its procedures for identifying candidates for trustee or trustee's counsel, and in so doing, to assess whether additional outreach efforts should be adopted and incorporated.

2. Advise SIPC to document its procedures and criteria for appointment of a trustee and trustee's counsel for its cases.

Agency and Third Party Comments and Our Evaluation

We provided a draft of this report to SEC, SIPC, and the Trustee for their review and comment, and we received written comments from SEC and SIPC, which are reprinted in appendixes IV and V, respectively. In their comments, SEC and SIPC concurred with our recommendations. The director of SEC's Division of Trading and Markets said the division will recommend that the SEC Chairman implement our recommendations. The SIPC President said SIPC will make plans to implement them immediately. Regarding documenting and assessing its outreach efforts for identifying trustee and trustee's counsel candidates, the SIPC

President said such efforts may lead to expansion of its file of potential service providers and thus allow SIPC to choose from a broader base. To achieve this, he indicated SIPC will explore expanding SIPC's contacts with relevant professional organizations, to locate qualified people and firms that SIPC has not previously encountered. Regarding documenting the process by which SIPC designates a trustee and trustee's counsel, the SIPC President's letter indicated that there is nothing in our recommendation that would delay or slow SIPC's progress, and that the need for transparency can be achieved as well. The SIPC President also said that in implementing both recommendations, SIPC will consult with SEC. SIPC, SEC, and the Trustee also provided technical comments, which we have incorporated as appropriate.

We are sending copies of this report to the appropriate congressional committees, the SEC Chairman, the SIPC President, and the Trustee for the Madoff liquidation. In addition, this report is available at no charge on the GAO website at http://www.gao.gov.

If you or your staff have any questions regarding this report, please contact me at (202)-512-8678 or clowersa@gao.gov. Contact points for our Offices of Congressional Relations and Public Affairs may be found on the last page of this report. GAO staff who made major contributions to this report are listed in appendix VI.

A. Nicole Clowers
Director
Financial Markets and
    Community Investment

Appendix I: Objectives, Scope, and Methodology

This report discusses (1) how the Trustee and trustee's counsel were selected for the Bernard L. Madoff Investment Securities, LLC liquidation; (2) the process and reasoning for the selection of "net investment method" (NIM) in determining customer claims arising from the Madoff fraud; (3) the costs of the subsequent liquidation of the Madoff firm; and (4) the information that the Trustee has disclosed about his investigation and activities.[1]

To examine how the Trustee and trustee's counsel were selected for the Madoff liquidation, we reviewed the requirements of the Securities Investor Protection Act (SIPA) for the selection of a trustee, plus court filings, correspondence and records of the Securities Investor Protection Corporation (SIPC), Standards for Internal Control in the Federal Government, the Internal Control – Integrated Framework of the Committee of Sponsoring Organizations of the Treadway Commission, biographical information for the Trustee, and relevant portions of the Bankruptcy Code. We also interviewed SIPC senior management, officials of the Securities and Exchange Commission (SEC) and the SEC Office of Inspector General (SEC IG), and the Trustee and members of the trustee's counsel law firm.

To examine the process and reasoning for the selection of NIM, we reviewed court filings, in particular those related to the Madoff fraud; and the Trustee's determination to use NIM, as well as a subsequent challenge to that decision. We examined SIPC correspondence and records, including information on open and closed SIPC cases (Ponzi scheme cases in particular), and customer claims under NIM and the final statement method (FSM). We also reviewed SIPC rules, annual reports, and board meeting minutes. We reviewed SEC correspondence and records, including consideration of net equity methods, arguments presented to the agency in support of FSM; and commission meeting minutes. We reviewed findings of the SEC IG. Additionally, we interviewed SIPC senior management, SEC officials, the SEC Inspector General, and the Trustee and members of the trustee's counsel law firm.

To examine the costs of the Madoff liquidation, we analyzed cost information from interim reports submitted by the Trustee to the

---

[1]The trustee in the Madoff liquidation is Irving H. Picard; the trustee's counsel is the law firm of Baker & Hostetler LLP.

bankruptcy court, covering the period from December 2008 to September 2011; cost requests submitted by the Trustee and trustee's counsel for approval by the bankruptcy court, covering the period from December 2008 through May 2011; and other records. We discussed with the Trustee, trustee's counsel, and SIPC their process for verifying costs submitted. Because this cost information is prepared for or approved by the bankruptcy court, we determined that no additional steps were necessary to assess its reliability and that this data was sufficiently reliable for our purposes of identifying total costs, cost components, and trends. We also reviewed SIPA provisions related to review and approval of legal costs, and SIPC guidance on trustee compensation and review of liquidation costs. We reviewed an American Bar Association model rule on the reasonability of legal fees, and an SEC IG report on SEC's oversight of SIPC costs. In addition, we interviewed SIPC senior management, SEC officials, the SEC IG, and the Trustee and members of the trustee's counsel law firm generally on the topic of Madoff liquidation costs.

To examine what information the Trustee has disclosed about his investigation and activities, we reviewed SIPA's disclosure requirements and the duties of trustees under chapter 7 of the Bankruptcy Code. We also reviewed court filings related to the Trustee's disclosures of information and his interim reports. We examined information the Trustee has made public about the investigation, including material on his website. In addition, we interviewed SIPC senior management, SEC officials, and the Trustee and members of the trustee's counsel law firm.

We conducted this performance audit from October 2011 to March 2012 in accordance with generally accepted government auditing standards. Those standards require that we plan and perform our audit to obtain sufficient, appropriate evidence to provide a reasonable basis for our findings and conclusions based on our audit objectives. We believe that the evidence obtained provides a reasonable basis for our findings and conclusions based on our audit objectives.

Appendix II: Securities Investor Protection Corporation Fund Assessments and Balances, 1990 to 2010

Since 1990, the Securities Investor Protection Corporation (SIPC) has assessed its member broker-dealers varying rates to support the fund used to protect customers of failed securities firms. Over this period, members have paid assessments to the fund based on different percentages of either their gross revenues or net operating revenues, or have paid a flat-rate amount.

Table 7: SIPC Fund Assessments and Balances, from 1990 to 2010

Year	SIPC member assessments and contributions	Assessment rate	Assessment basis	SIPC fund at December 31
1990	$73,029,832	0.001875	Gross revenue	$568,587,250
1991	38,851,496	0.00065	Net operating revenue	678,769,209
1992	27,217,374	0.00057	Net operating revenue	720,214,522
1993	32,612,767	0.00054	Net operating revenue	791,366,865
1994	37,115,454	0.00073	Net operating revenue	867,152,034
1995	57,831,365	0.00095	Net operating revenue	965,932,279
1996	2,639,822	$150	Flat	1,047,205,945
1997	1,339,584	$150	Flat	1,109,450,764
1998	1,186,279	$150	Flat	1,196,695,240
1999	1,136,318	$150	Flat	1,129,653,262
2000	1,108,632	$150	Flat	1,220,284,553
2001	1,083,173	$150	Flat	1,184,157,015
2002	1,050,096	$150	Flat	1,260,200,497
2003	1,083,178	$150	Flat	1,249,116,852
2004	972,817	$150	Flat	1,287,554,216
2005	927,597	$150	Flat	1,286,092,231
2006	894,941	$150	Flat	1,403,558,035
2007	852,025	$150	Flat	1,522,257,439
2008	816,322	$150	Flat	1,699,039,958
2009	346,299,978	0.0025	Net operating revenue	1,091,831,811
2010	409,200,016	0.0025	Net operating revenue	1,181,851,883

Source: SIPC.

Appendix III: Legal Appendix on Determination of Net Equity

Customer claims in a Securities Investor Protection Act (SIPA) liquidation are based on customers' "net equity" as of the filing date (Dec. 11, 2008, in the Madoff case). The statute generally provides that net equity is what would have been owed to the customer if the broker-dealer had liquidated the customer's "securities positions," less any obligations of the customer to the firm. Overall, each customer's net equity determines the value of each claim. In particular, it determines their pro rata share from the customer property portion of the insolvent broker-dealer's estate, as well as the amount of any advance payment from the Securities Investor Protection Corporation (SIPC) fund to which the customer may be entitled.[1]

The Trustee chose the "net investment method" (NIM), which focuses on investments made and not profits reported, to determine net equity. Claimants challenged the method, and it was upheld first by the U.S. Bankruptcy Court for the Southern District of New York.[2] Later, the U.S. Court of Appeals for the Second Circuit affirmed the bankruptcy court decision.[3] In the following sections, we describe the Trustee's position, the positions of the other parties, and the two judicial decisions.

The Parties Advocated for Two Different Net Equity Methods, and the Trustee Determined That NIM Was Proper

The issue of how to determine net equity in the Madoff case primarily involved a choice between two methods with different impacts on the two main classes of customers. As is generally true of Ponzi scheme frauds, the Madoff claimants were "net winners" or "net losers." The net winners were those customers who had withdrawn the full cash amount they had invested in the Madoff firm before its collapse, plus some "profit" (that is, fictitious gains that actually came from funds provided for investment by others). The net losers were customers who had paid in more than they had withdrawn at the time the Madoff firm collapsed.[4]

---

[1]SIPA authorizes an advance payment of up to $500,000 from SIPC to customers with approved claims.

[2]*Securities Investor Protection Corp. v. Bernard L. Madoff Investment Securities LLC* (*In re Bernard L. Madoff Investment Securities LLC*), 424 B.R. 122 (Bankr. S.D.N.Y. 2010).

[3]*In re Bernard L. Madoff Investment Securities LLC*, 654 F.3d 229 (2d Cir. 2011).

[4]The bankruptcy court noted that, in general, the net winners were concentrated among early Madoff investors, while most net losers were later investors. 424 B.R. at 132.

The two competing methods for calculating net equity were NIM and the
"final statement method" (FSM).[5] NIM calculates what customers are
owed as the amounts they invested, less amounts withdrawn. FSM
calculates net equity based on the amounts shown as customers'
securities positions on the last statements received from the broker-
dealer firm; in the Madoff case, as of November 30, 2008.[6]

SIPC and the Securities and Exchange Commission (SEC) both
supported the Trustee's selection of NIM.[7] A number of claimants argued
for use of FSM. These claimants, most of whom were net winners,[8]
challenged the Trustee's choice of NIM.

Both Sides Claimed the Law Supported Their Position

The legal arguments of the parties are reflected in the bankruptcy court
and Court of Appeals opinions. In addition, the bankruptcy court opinion
included an exhibit that outlined the competing arguments in detail.[9]

The issue of how to determine net equity in the Madoff case turned on
two key SIPA provisions: One is the definition of "net equity" in section
16(11) of the act, which generally requires the trustee to determine a
customer's net equity by "calculating the sum which would have been
owed by the [broker-dealer] debtor to such customer if the debtor had
liquidated, by sale or purchase on the filing date . . . *all securities
positions* of such customer . . . minus . . . any indebtedness of such
customer to the debtor on the filing date . . ." (emphasis added).[10]

---

[5]NIM is also known as the "cash in/cash out" or "money in/money out" method, and FSM
as the "last statement method."

[6]As described earlier in this report, the Securities and Exchange Commission also
considered other methods. However, the two basic methods were NIM and FSM,
according to our review.

[7]SEC's position differed from the Trustee's in one respect. SEC advocated adding an
inflation adjustment to customers' NIM claims, to compensate them for the time value of
their money. It referred to this as the "constant dollar approach." See 424 B.R. at 125, n.
8. Neither the bankruptcy court nor the Court of Appeals have addressed the merits of the
SEC position thus far.

[8]424 B.R. at 132, n. 24.

[9]*Id.* at 144-153.

[10]15 U.S.C. § 78lll(16).

The other is section 8(b) of the act, which requires the Trustee to determine net equity claims "insofar as such obligations are ascertainable from the books and records of the debtor or are otherwise established to the satisfaction of the trustee."[11]

The Trustee, supported by SIPC and SEC, took the position that because the statements customers received from the Madoff firm were fictitious, they did not show "securities positions" that could be relied upon for purposes of the net equity determination. Instead, the only Madoff firm records that reflected reality were those recording the cash deposits and withdrawals of customers. Thus, the Trustee argued, the plain language of section 8(b) required the trustee to determine net equity based on these records, since they provided the only obligations that could be established from the Madoff firm's books and records. Accordingly, in his view, NIM was the only legally permissible option.

The Trustee also contended that fairness considerations strongly supported use of NIM. Using FSM would exacerbate Madoff's fraud and enable some Madoff customers to retain "profits" that were in reality the misappropriated investments of other customers. Moreover, FSM would divert the limited customer assets available in the bankrupt estate by paying imaginary "profits" at the expense of reimbursing real losses. The Trustee also argued that using FSM could conflict with his obligation to recover the fictitious profits paid out by the Madoff firm through avoidance actions.[12]

The claimants advocating use of FSM argued that the plain language of section 16(11) required use of this method, because the Madoff firm statements reflected securities positions they had every reason to believe were accurate and on which that they had relied. They emphasized SIPA's purpose to reinforce investor confidence in securities markets. In particular, they cited the following passage from SIPA's legislative history as indicating that securities positions set forth in broker-dealer statements need not be accurate in order to be relied upon under the act:

[11]15 U.S.C. § 78fff-2(b).

[12]Avoidance actions, sometimes referred to as "clawbacks," enable a bankruptcy trustee to recover for the bankrupt estate certain payments made by the debtor prior to the bankruptcy filing.

"*What The Customer Gets.* A customer generally expects to receive what he believes is in his account at the time the stockbroker ceases business. But because securities may have been lost, improperly hypothecated, misappropriated, never purchased or even stolen, this is not always possible. Accordingly, when the customer claims for a particular stock exceed the supply available to the trustee in the debtor's estate, then customers generally receive pro rata portions of the securities claims, and as to any remainder, they will receive cash based on the market value as of the filing date."[13]

FSM advocates also argued that the profits Madoff reported, while fictitious, may have been withdrawn and spent years ago; that customers paid taxes on them; and they may have foregone other investment opportunities in reliance on investment results shown in their statements.

Furthermore, they maintained that, at least in the case of advances from the SIPC fund, use of FSM would not limit payments to reimburse net losers for their losses. They viewed the SIPC fund as a payment source for customer claims that operated separately and independently from any customer assets in the bankrupt estate. Thus, all claimants, both net winners and losers, could potentially receive up to $500,000 from the SIPC fund without any decrease in customer property.

Finally, both sides contended that judicial precedent dealing with SIPA liquidations involving Ponzi scheme cases (discussed in the following section) supported their calculation method.

---

[13]H.R. Rep. No. 95-746, 21 (1977), the House report on the legislation enacted as the 1978 amendments to SIPA. The context for the quoted passage is a 1978 amendment, now section 8(b)(2) of SIPA, 15 U.S.C. § 78fff-2(b)(2), authorizing trustees to satisfy claims (in lieu of cash payments) by purchasing and delivering securities to replace those ascertainable from a customer's account.

The Bankruptcy Court Affirmed the Trustee's Selection of NIM

The bankruptcy court affirmed the Trustee's determination of net equity method and essentially sided with the Trustee, SIPC, and SEC on each of their key arguments. The court concluded:

> "The Court recognizes that the application of the Net Equity definition to the complex and unique facts of Madoff's massive Ponzi scheme is not plainly ascertainable in law. Indeed, the parties have advanced compelling arguments in support of both positions. Ultimately, however, upon a thorough and comprehensive analysis of the plain meaning and legislative history of the statute, controlling Second Circuit precedent, and considerations of equity and practicality, the Court endorses the Trustee's Net Investment Method."[14]

Specifically, the court agreed with the Trustee that sections 16(11) and 8(b) of the act must be read together, so that net equity can be based on "securities positions" only to the extent that securities positions are "ascertainable from the books and records of the debtor" or "otherwise established to the satisfaction of the trustee." The court further agreed that in a Ponzi scheme case like the Madoff fraud, where no securities were ever ordered or acquired, securities positions did not exist, and the Trustee cannot satisfy claims by relying upon fictitious account statements that provided fictitious securities positions. Instead, only cash deposits and withdrawals were verifiable from the books and records of the Madoff firm.[15] The court added that legitimate customer expectations based on false account statements "do not apply where they would give rise to an absurd result."[16]

The bankruptcy court also found that fairness favored NIM. It concluded that payments from the SIPC fund were inextricably connected to payments from customer property, rejecting the argument by FSM proponents to the contrary. Thus, use of FSM for purposes of SIPC fund advance payments would in fact diminish the amount available for

---

[14]424 B.R. at 125.

[15]*Id.* at 135.

[16]*Id.*

distribution from the customer property fund. Citing section 9(a)(1) of the act,[17] the court observed:

> "SIPC payments therefore serve only to replace missing customer property and cannot be ascertained independently of the determination of the customer's *pro rata* share of customer property. Accordingly, the SIPA statute does not allow bifurcation of the claims process, with customers recovering SIPC payments based on the [Final] Statement Method, and recovering customer property shares based on the Net Investment Method."[18]

Viewing fairness considerations from this perspective, the bankruptcy court stated:

> "While the Court recognizes that the outcome of this dispute will inevitably be unpalatable to one party or another, notions of fairness and the need for practicality also support the Net Investment Method."

> "As distribution of customer property to the 'equally innocent victims' of Madoff's fraud is a zero-sum game, equity dictates that the Court implement the Net Investment Method. Customer property consists of a limited amount of funds that are available for distribution. Any dollar paid to reimburse a fictitious profit is a dollar no longer available to pay claims for money actually invested. If the [Final] Statement Method were adopted, Net Winners would receive more favorable treatment by profiting from the principal investments of Net Losers, yielding an inequitable result."[19]

---

[17]15 U.S.C. § 78fff-3(a)(1): "In order to provide for prompt payment and satisfaction of net equity claims of customers of the debtor, SIPC shall advance to the trustee such moneys, not to exceed $500,000 for each customer, *as may be required to pay or otherwise satisfy claims for the amount by which the net equity of each customer exceeds his ratable share of customer property . . .*" (emphasis added by the court). 424 B.R. at 134.

[18]424 B.R. at 134.

[19]*Id.* at 140-141 (footnote and citation omitted).

The bankruptcy court also agreed with the Trustee that NIM was more compatible with trustee avoidance powers under the Bankruptcy Code.

"The Trustee relies on numerous cases, all holding that transfers made in furtherance of a Ponzi scheme, and specifically transfers of fictitious profits, are avoidable. The Net Investment Method harmonizes the definition of Net Equity with these avoidance provisions by similarly discrediting transfers of purely fictitious amounts and unwinding, rather than legitimizing, the fraudulent scheme. The [Final] Statement Method, by contrast, would create tension within the statute by centering distribution to customers on the very fictitious transfers the Trustee has the power to avoid."[20]

Finally, the bankruptcy court concluded that judicial precedent involving Ponzi scheme cases, including *In re New Times Securities Services, Inc.*, supported use of NIM in the Madoff liquidation.[21] *New Times* also concerned a SIPA liquidation arising out of a Ponzi scheme fraud.

In *New Times*, some investors (known as "real securities claimants") had been offered shares in real mutual funds, which the Ponzi schemer-debtor never purchased. Other investors (known as "fake securities claimants") purchased shares in fictitious money market funds with fictitious names. The debtor generated monthly statements for both sets of investors that showed fictitious securities positions as well as interest and dividend earnings. The SIPA trustee in *New Times* treated the two sets of investors differently. He determined that for those investors whose fictitious statements reflected the purchase of real securities, their net equity for purposes of the act should be based on the positions shown in their statements—that is, he applied FSM. (This treatment was not before the court in *New Times*.) However, the trustee determined that for investors whose statements reflected earnings from the entirely fictitious funds, their net equity was limited to their initial investments—that is, he applied NIM to them.[22]

---

[20]*Id.* at 136 (footnote omitted). The bankruptcy court noted that no specific avoidance actions were before it at the time and thus expressed no view on the merits of potential defenses to them. *Id.* at 136-137.

[21]371 F.3d 68 (2d Cir. 2004). This decision is often referred to as "*New Times I*" because of a somewhat related subsequent decision, *In re New Times Securities Services, Inc.*, 463 F.3d 125 (2d Cir. 2006) ("*New Times II*").

[22]The principal issue addressed in *New Times I* was whether the fake securities claimants had claims for cash or claims for securities. This question has not been raised in the Madoff litigation, and therefore we do not discuss that aspect of the *New Times I* decision.

The fake securities claimants appealed the trustee's determinations to the federal district court. The district court sided with the investors, holding that their net equity should be calculated using FSM, recognizing the fictitious interest and dividend reinvestment earnings shown on their statements. The SIPA trustee then appealed the district court's decision. SEC joined SIPC in maintaining that NIM should be used to determine the fictitious fund investors' net equity.

On appeal, the Court of Appeals for the Second Circuit endorsed the joint position of SIPC and SEC that net equity of the fake securities claimants should be based solely on their initial investments, excluding imaginary interest and dividends shown on the statements. The appeals court agreed that basing recoveries on fictitious interest and dividend amounts would be "irrational and unworkable."[23]

In the Madoff litigation, both parties argued that *New Times* supported their position. The Madoff net winners argued they should be compared to the first group of *New Times* customers, who were supposedly invested in real mutual funds, because Madoff's account statements showed positions in real securities. Because the real securities claimants in *New Times* had their net equity calculated by FSM, Madoff net winners argued they should likewise have their net equity calculated by FSM.

Instead, the bankruptcy court endorsed the position of the Trustee, SIPC, and SEC by analogizing Madoff net winners to the fake securities claimants in *New Times* with their fictitious holdings, which led to NIM as the appropriate method by which to calculate their net equity.[24] The court explained that the key precedent set by *New Times* regarding net equity analysis is that customer recovery cannot be based on account statements that contain numbers with no relation to reality, whether the securities are identifiable by name (as in Madoff) or not (as in *New Times*).[25] Reliance on fraudulent promises in account statements, the court stated, would create "the absurdity of 'duped' investors reaping

---

[23]371 F.3d at 88.

[24]The bankruptcy court also considered *New Times II*, 463 F.3d 125, as well as another Ponzi scheme case, *In re Old Naples Securities, Inc.*, 311 B.R. 607 (M.D. Fl. 2002), which likewise rejected inclusion of fictitious interest earnings in SIPA net equity.

[25]424 B.R. at 139.

windfalls as a result of fraudulent promises."[26] The court also noted that the initial investments of real securities claimants in *New Times* were sufficient to acquire their initial securities, and subsequent statements listing earnings reflected actual market events. By contrast, initial investments by Madoff investors were "insufficient to acquire their purported securities positions, which were made possible only by virtue of fictitious profits . . . [as] account activity was manipulated with the benefit of deliberately calibrated hindsight."[27]

The Court of Appeals Affirmed the Bankruptcy Court's Decision

The Court of Appeals for the Second Circuit reviewed the bankruptcy court's ruling on net equity in the Madoff case on a *de novo* basis.[28] It affirmed the bankruptcy court decision, holding that while SIPA does not prescribe a single method for determining net equity in all situations—

"Mr. Picard's selection of the Net Investment Method was more consistent with the statutory definition of 'net equity' than any other method advocated by the parties or perceived by this Court. There was therefore no error. . . . The statutory definition of 'net equity' does not require the Trustee to aggravate the injuries caused by Madoff's fraud. Use of the [Final] Statement Method in this case would have the absurd effect of treating fictitious and arbitrarily assigned paper profits as real and would give legal effect to Madoff's machinations."[29]

---

[26]*Id.* (citing *New Times II*, 463 F.3d at 130).

[27]*Id.*

[28]A *de novo* review gives no deference to the lower court's rulings.

[29]654 F.3d at 235.

The Court of Appeals endorsed the reasoning of the bankruptcy court. At the same time, it emphasized:

> "In holding that it was proper for Mr. Picard to reject the [Final] Statement Method, we expressly do not hold that such a method of calculating 'net equity' is inherently impermissible. To the contrary, a customer's last account statement will likely be the most appropriate means of calculating 'net equity' in more conventional cases. We would expect that resort to the Net Investment Method would be rare because this method wipes out all events of a customer's investment history except for cash deposits and withdrawals. The extraordinary facts of this case make the Net Investment Method appropriate whereas in many instances, it would not be. The [Final] Statement Method, for example, may be appropriate when securities were actually purchased by the debtor, but then converted by the debtor."[30]

The Court of Appeals also rejected the FSM advocates' characterization of SIPA as providing "an insurance guarantee of the securities positions set out in their account statements" which should "operate to make them whole from the losses they incurred as a result of Madoff's dishonesty."[31] On the contrary, the Court of Appeals observed that SIPA did not necessarily protect against all forms of fraud committed by brokers or insure investors against all losses.

Legal Issues Remain

The U.S. Court of Appeals for the Second Circuit has affirmed the Trustee's use of NIM, but several legal issues remain. Courts have yet to rule on whether calculations of net equity under NIM should include an adjustment for inflation. A ruling supporting this "constant dollar" approach would stand to affect liquidation payouts for a significant number of Madoff customers. In addition, the Trustee is pursuing a large number of actions against Madoff net winners—known as clawbacks or avoidance actions—seeking to recover assets they received that exceeded their investments. The outcome of these actions likewise will affect liquidation payouts to Madoff customers. Finally, petitions seeking review of the appeals court's net equity ruling have been filed with the U.S. Supreme Court.

---

[30]*Id.* at 238.

[31]*Id.* at 239.

Appendix IV: Comments from the Securities and Exchange Commission

UNITED STATES
SECURITIES AND EXCHANGE COMMISSION
WASHINGTON, DC 20549

DIVISION OF
TRADING AND MARKETS

March 2, 2012

A. Nicole Clowers
Director
Financial Markets and Community Investment
United States Government Accountability Office
441 G Street, NW
Washington, DC 20548

Dear Ms. Clowers:

Thank you for the opportunity to comment on the Government Accountability Office's draft report *Securities Investor Protection Corporation: Interim Report on the Madoff Liquidation Proceeding* ("Draft Report"). We have reviewed the Draft Report and have sent to your staff certain technical comments.

The Draft Report makes two recommendations to improve SIPC's process for selecting trustees. First, the Draft Report recommends that the SEC Chairman advise SIPC to document its procedures for identifying candidates to serve as trustee or as trustee's counsel and to assess whether additional outreach efforts should be adopted and incorporated. In addition, the Draft Report recommends that the SEC Chairman advise SIPC to document its procedures and criteria for appointing a trustee and a trustee's counsel for each liquidation. The Division of Trading and Markets staff will recommend that the Chairman take these actions.

Thank you for the opportunity to comment on the Draft Report.

Sincerely,

Robert W. Cook
Director

Appendix V: Comments from the Securities Investor Protection Corporation

SECURITIES INVESTOR PROTECTION CORPORATION
805 FIFTEENTH STREET, N. W., SUITE 800
WASHINGTON, D. C. 20005-2215
(202) 371-8300   FAX (202) 371-6728
WWW.SIPC.ORG

February 28, 2012

<u>**By Hand Delivery and E-mail**</u>

A. Nicole Clowers
Director
Financial Markets and Community Investment
U.S. Government Accountability Office
441 G St NW
Washington, DC 20548

RE: <u>**SIPC Interim Report on the Madoff Liquidation Proceeding**</u>

Dear Ms. Clowers:

Thank you for the opportunity to review and comment upon the GAO Report entitled SECURITIES INVESTOR PROTECTION CORPORATION INTERIM REPORT ON THE MADOFF LIQUIDATION PROCEEDING. SIPC's staff has reviewed the Report and offers the following comments.

Any report of this nature offers the prospect of reviewing and improving the work of the organization that is the subject of the examination, and the current report is no exception. The Interim Report makes two recommendations, and SIPC will make plans to implement those recommendations immediately.

Documenting and Assessing the "Outreach" Procedure for Service Providers

First, the GAO recommends that SIPC document its procedures for identifying service providers and assess whether additional outreach efforts are necessary to extend the prospective talent pool of persons who are qualified to serve in SIPC cases. We are pleased that the Interim Report recognizes the need to move swiftly when SIPC is notified of a brokerage firm failure. Implementing this recommendation may lead to the expansion of our existing database of possible service providers and thus allow SIPC to choose from a broader base of persons with the requisite capabilities.

Ms. A. Nicole Clowers
February 28, 2012
Page 2

Initial thoughts on this matter include expanding SIPC's contacts and participation with organizations such as the American Bankruptcy Institute, the National Conference of Bankruptcy Judges, and the National Association of Bankruptcy Trustees. Individuals and firms which SIPC has not previously encountered, but which have the necessary skill sets, can be located through these organizations.

Finally, SIPC will consult with the SEC staff to discuss any procedures the Commission currently uses to document and maintain an outreach for potential Receivers in various types of SEC proceedings.

Documenting the Process by which SIPC Designates a Trustee and Counsel at the Outset of a Customer Protection Proceeding

Second, the GAO recommends that SIPC document the process by which SIPC designates a trustee and counsel when a customer protection proceeding needs to be initiated. Once again, I believe the Interim Report correctly recognizes the need for virtually immediate action. There is nothing in the recommendation that would delay or slow SIPC's progress in any way, and the SIPC staff agrees that the need for transparency can be accommodated as well. Among the items that could be documented, contemporaneously, are:

- The prospective size of the engagement, if known, so as to assure that the service providers chosen have adequate resources;
- Whether the engagement is one which is sufficiently limited in scope to introduce a new service provider to a SIPA proceeding or whether the engagement necessitates a proven service provider;
- The specific process used by the service provider to discover possible conflicts of interest;
- Any specific agreement by a service provider to provide a "public service discount" from the ordinary rates;
- Any unique problems presented by the referral from the SEC or self-regulatory organization, which might require specialized expertise.
- The persons within the SIPC staff who were consulted with respect to the engagement

Over time, I am sure the SIPC staff will be able to develop other criteria that would be useful in this regard.

Also, as with the first recommendation, SIPC will consult with the SEC staff to discuss any procedures the SEC uses to document the process of choosing an SEC Receiver, since the designation of a Receiver by the SEC and the designation of a Trustee and Counsel by SIPC are clearly analogous.

Ms. A. Nicole Clowers
February 28, 2012
Page 3

Other Matters Addressed by the Interim Report.

While the Interim Report touches on a wide variety of SIPC's work in the <u>Madoff</u> case, I wanted to point out two matters in particular where the document makes very important findings.

First, the Interim Report notes (page 29) that the costs of the Madoff liquidation are driven by efforts to recover assets for customers. This is absolutely correct, and an important point that needs to be emphasized to the public. SIPC and the Trustee agree that cost containment is important. But maximizing the return to victimized claimants takes precedence.

Second, with respect to the issue of how to measure the correct value of any customer claim in the Madoff case, I note that the Interim Report correctly states (page 22) that neither SIPC, nor the SEC, not the Trustee, took the cost to SIPC of any particular methodology into account. Instead, as both the Bankruptcy Court and the Second Circuit Court of Appeals noted, using the so-called Final Statement methodology in this instance has the absurd effect of legitimizing the arbitrarily assigned paper profits that the Madoff fraud produced. (The Interim Report notes the Courts' conclusions at page 25.) The use of a Final Statement methodology would, as a simple matter of arithmetic, diminish the returns to those most harmed by Madoff's theft, to wit, those persons who did not receive all of their initial deposits with the Madoff firm.

Going Forward.

Both the "Interim" title of the Report, and footnote 2 therein, indicate that the GAO will continue to study this matter. I hope this letter indicates that SIPC has both taken your recommendations to heart and looks forward to your input in the future.

Very truly yours,

Stephen P. Harbeck
President and CEO

Appendix VI: GAO Contact and Staff Acknowledgments

GAO Contact	A. Nicole Clowers, (202) 512-8678 or clowersa@gao.gov
Staff Acknowledgments	In addition to the contact named above, Cody J. Goebel, Assistant Director; Rachel DeMarcus; Dean P. Gudicello; Daniel S. Kaneshiro; Jonathan M. Kucskar; Marc W. Molino, Barbara M. Roesmann; and Christopher H. Schmitt made major contributions to this report.

GAO's Mission	The Government Accountability Office, the audit, evaluation, and investigative arm of Congress, exists to support Congress in meeting its constitutional responsibilities and to help improve the performance and accountability of the federal government for the American people. GAO examines the use of public funds; evaluates federal programs and policies; and provides analyses, recommendations, and other assistance to help Congress make informed oversight, policy, and funding decisions. GAO's commitment to good government is reflected in its core values of accountability, integrity, and reliability.
Obtaining Copies of GAO Reports and Testimony	The fastest and easiest way to obtain copies of GAO documents at no cost is through GAO's website (www.gao.gov). Each weekday afternoon, GAO posts on its website newly released reports, testimony, and correspondence. To have GAO e-mail you a list of newly posted products, go to www.gao.gov and select "E-mail Updates."
Order by Phone	The price of each GAO publication reflects GAO's actual cost of production and distribution and depends on the number of pages in the publication and whether the publication is printed in color or black and white. Pricing and ordering information is posted on GAO's website, http://www.gao.gov/ordering.htm. Place orders by calling (202) 512-6000, toll free (866) 801-7077, or TDD (202) 512-2537. Orders may be paid for using American Express, Discover Card, MasterCard, Visa, check, or money order. Call for additional information.
Connect with GAO	Connect with GAO on Facebook, Flickr, Twitter, and YouTube. Subscribe to our RSS Feeds or E-mail Updates. Listen to our Podcasts. Visit GAO on the web at www.gao.gov.
To Report Fraud, Waste, and Abuse in Federal Programs	Contact: Website: www.gao.gov/fraudnet/fraudnet.htm E-mail: fraudnet@gao.gov Automated answering system: (800) 424-5454 or (202) 512-7470
Congressional Relations	Katherine Siggerud, Managing Director, siggerudk@gao.gov, (202) 512-4400, U.S. Government Accountability Office, 441 G Street NW, Room 7125, Washington, DC 20548
Public Affairs	Chuck Young, Managing Director, youngc1@gao.gov, (202) 512-4800 U.S. Government Accountability Office, 441 G Street NW, Room 7149 Washington, DC 20548

Please Print on Recycled Paper.

www.ingramcontent.com/pod-product-compliance
Lightning Source LLC
Chambersburg PA
CBHW081138290526
45795CB00006B/2281